Cooking with Trader Joe's

Cookbook

Vegetarian

Deana Gunn & Wona Minati

Cooking with Trader Joe's Cookbook: Vegetarian
by Deana Gunn and Wona Miniati
Photographs by Deana Gunn and Wona Miniati
Designed by Lilla Hangay
Produced by Deana Gunn and Wona Miniati

Published by Brown Bag Publishers, LLC
P.O. Box 235065
Encinitas, CA 92023
info@cookTJ.com

Printed in China through Overseas Printing Corporation

Library of Congress Cataloging-in-Publication Data
Gunn, Deana and Miniati, Wona
Cooking with Trader Joe's Cookbook: Vegetarian/
by Deana Gunn and Wona Miniati; photographs by Deana Gunn and Wona Miniati – 1st ed.
Includes index.

I. Quick and easy cookery. 2. Trader Joe's (Store) I. Title.

ISBN   978-1-938706-01-1   1938706013

Table of Contents

Thank You Notes	5
Introduction	6

Appetizers — 10

Apricot Baked Brie	13
Roasted Garlic (Friends Be Damned)	14
Homemade Hummus	16
Indian Spinach Pizza	17
Tomato and Mozzarella Skewers	19
Pisto Manchego	20
Olive-Stuffed Bread	23
Just Peachy Dip	24
Cheese & Chutney Mini-Rolls	25
California Caviar (Bean Salsa)	26
Ten-Layer Mexican Dip	28
Warm Honeyed Figs with Goat Cheese	31
Creamy Stuffed Mushroom Caps	32
Kickin' Artichoke Dip	35
Strawberry Mango Salsa	36

Soups & Salads — 38

Endive, Beet and Avocado Salad	41
Italian Wedding Soup	42
Wasabi Tofu Salad	44
Hearts and Snaps Salad	46
Mediterranean Lentil Salad	47
Black Bean Soup	48
Nutty Wild Rice Salad	51
Asian Dumpling Soup	52
Posh Mâche Salad	55
Warm Goat Cheese Salad	56
Life is a Bowl of Cherries, Pine Nuts, and Spinach Salad	59
Green Waldorf Salad	60
Le French Lentil Soup	63
Egg Salad Olovieh (Persian Egg Salad)	64
Can't Beet It Mandarin Orange Salad	66
Notcho Ordinary Gazpacho	68
Arugula Salad with Pine Nuts and Parmesan	69
Harvest Grains Vegetable Soup	70
Homemade Blue Cheese Dressing	72
Winter Caprese (Beet and Mozzarella Salad)	75

Main Meals — 76

Stuffed Red Peppers	78
Pasta alla Checca	81
Black Bean Burger	82
Hurry for Curry	85
Portabella Bunless Burger	86
Grilled Veggie Sandwich with Lemon Garlic Sauce	89
Thai Pizza	90
Corny-Copia Bean and Veggie Casserole	92
Portabella "Philly Cheesesteak"	94
Boursin Roasted Red Pepper Penne	97
Vegetable Tikka Masala	98
Anytime Mediterranean Pasta	101
Roasted Red Pepper and Mozzarella Sandwich	102
Easy Tofu Stir Fry	104
Stir-Fried Pasta with Sun Dried Tomatoes	106
Creamy Lemony Linguine	109
Soy Chorizo Chili	110
Southwest Burrito	113
Pesto Pita Pizza	114
Spicy Szechuan Tofu	117
Simply Quiche	118
Shiitake Mushroom Risotto	121
Eggplant Parmesan	122
Tamale Bake	125
Sushi Bowl	126
No-Prep Veggie Lasagna	128
Spinach Pesto Pasta Salad	131
Mushroom Moussaka	132
Black Bean and Ricotta-Stuffed Portabellas	135

South of the Border Pizza 136
Gyoza Salad 138
Gnutmeg Gnocchi with Spinach 141
Five-Minute Shiitake Fried Rice 142
Hummus and Lentil Wrap 145
White Lightning Chili 147
Addictive Tacos 148
Grilled Lentil Wraps 150
Spinach Ricotta Calzone 153
My Big Fat Greek Quiche 155
Mozzarella Basil Wrap 156
Arugula Pesto Pasta 159
Peanutty Sesame Noodles 160

Sides 162

Roasted Asparagus with Tomatoes and Feta 165
Black Bean Cornbread 166
Eggplant Zucchini Bake 167
Crunchy Broccoli Slaw 169
Balsamic Roasted Fennel 170
Coconut Curried Vegetables 171
Oven Roasted Vegetables with Rosemary 172
Baked Sweet Potato Fries 174
Roasted Cauliflower with Olives 177
Loco for Coconut Rice 178
Pan-Toasted Brussels Sprouts 181
Couscous with Sun Dried Tomatoes 182
Sesame Toasted Sugar Snap peas 185
Almond Bread 187

Desserts & Drinks 188

Honey, I Ate the Chocolate Bread Pudding 191
Low-Fat Wide Awake Coffee Shake 192
Lemon Basil Cake 193
Monkey Bread 194
Chocolate Truffle Pie with Joe-Joe's Crust 197
All Mixed Up Margaritas 198
Chocolate Lava Cake 200
Chia Energy Drink (Chia Fresca) 203
One Bowl Peach & Blueberry Cobbler 204

Simple Apple Tart 207
Orange Creamsicle Smoothie 208
Very Berry Mascarpone Tart 210
Lemon Drop Martini 213
No Moo Mousse 214
Good-for-you Strawberries and Cream 216
Mango Lassi 217
Frozen Tiramisu 218
Almond Pudding 221
Nearly Instant Homemade Mango Ice Cream 222
Vanilla Chai Bread Pudding 225
Lemon Tart with Fresh Berries 226
Peachy Sangria 227
Chocolate Coffee Fudge 229
"A Hint of Coffee" Brownies with Café Latte Glaze 230
Mighty Mojito 233

Breakfast 234

Super-Food Fruit Smoothie 236
Goat Cheese Scramble 238
Quick and Creamy Quinoa Cereal 241
Yogurt Parfait 243
Swiss Muesli 244
Veggie Masala Scramble 247
Baked French Toast Casserole 248
Mushroom Basil Frittata 251
Purple Porridge 252
Orange Cranberry Scones 255

Index 256
Gluten-Free Index 262
Trader Joe's Store Locations 263

Thank You Notes

A heartfelt thanks to our family and friends who continue to cheer us on as we enthusiastically create more cookbooks starring our favorite store.

We praise our talented designer Lilla Hangay for making each book more beautiful and fun than the one before. We thank our editor Heather World for polishing our prose and helping us say all them thar words in the goodest way.

Many thanks to our customers who share their feedback and favorite recipes with us. We love hearing from you, and your kind emails and calls make our day. In fact, you are the inspiration behind this cookbook. In 2011, we published *Cooking with Trader Joe's: Skinny Dish!*, a vegan cookbook that became an instant hit. "But wait," said all our vegetarian fans, "...what about us??" You asked for our best vegetarian recipes all in one place, and here they are (with a few new recipes added in)!

A big shout-out to Trader Joe's, our favorite store in the whole wide world. We can't imagine a better place to shop or nicer crewmembers to greet us as we cruise the aisles.

We thank you all!

Introduction

Years ago, we had the idea to create something new: a Trader Joe's cookbook. It was the perfect way to share all our original recipes and cooking ideas that helped us create meals easily and quickly every night of the week. The idea was simple: make Trader Joe's our one-stop shop and use their time-saving products in our recipes. For years, we had shopped the aisles, created recipes around what we saw, stocked up on our favorite products, and fantasized about how to use new products. We strategized about all the shortcuts that would cut our cooking time in a fraction of what it would be if we did everything the old-fashioned, from-scratch way. The cookbook was a resounding hit, because it turns out that we weren't the only ones looking for delicious, easy meals made in a snap.

A Vegetarian Trader Joe's Cookbook

Both of us naturally lean towards vegetarian fare, and we love the challenge of creating vegetarian dishes that are delicious, satisfying, and complete.

Deana only recently turned omnivore, having spent decades cooking from the well-worn, splattered pages of iconic cookbooks like Moosewood Restaurant and Vegetarian Times. (Ok, she sometimes cheated with bacon.) Living in big cities like Boston, Chicago, and Los Angeles always guaranteed easy access to vegetarian restaurants with interesting new dishes. Her vegetarian roots are evident in her everyday cooking, from dishes like black bean soup to meatless chili to stuffed Portabellas. On the flip side, Wona is a lifelong omnivore, but her husband went vegetarian just last year. She soon learned to balance her plate with plant proteins and whip up vegetarian versions of gourmet favorites.

After we published the vegan cookbook *Cooking with Trader Joe's: Skinny Dish!*, our fans clamored for a vegetarian cookbook. We began to assemble a collection of our favorite recipes from the **Cooking with Trader Joe's** series. Thus was born a vegetarian cookbook for the Trader Joe's shopper—a cookbook that won't leave you skipping recipes or wondering how you can substitute ingredients to create a vegetarian version of a meat dish. Most of these recipes are collected from the other cookbooks in our series, though some have been created especially for this book.

Why Vegetarian?

Vegetarian eating has been popular for ... well, for as long as we can remember. Why? The reasons are many and varied, but the top three typically are:

1. Health.
According to the American Dietetic Association, vegetarians have a lower risk of heart disease, obesity, colon cancer, and other cancers. Vegetarians also have lower cholesterol levels, lower blood pressure, lower body mass index, and lower rates of type 2 diabetes. The ADA's position is that well-planned vegetarian diets are healthful, adequate, and appropriate for all stages of life. The United States Department of Agriculture recently praised the vegetarian diet, noting similar health benefits.

2. Ethics and animal cruelty.
Many vegetarians object to killing an animal for the sake of food when there are so many other options. Others decry the inhumane conditions that seem to prevail on the commercial farms and in slaughterhouses of the meat industry.

3. Impact on the environment.
Livestock farms (and farms for the grain grown to feed the livestock) drain biological and chemical waste that pollutes nearby land, streams, and rivers. Additionally, our atmosphere suffers when rainforests are cut down to make way for cattle farms. Acre for acre, land is used much more efficiently to grow plant-based food than to raise meat.

Our aim is not to convince you of whether or why you should eat vegetarian. You, your doctor, and your philosophical beliefs are the best judge of that. Our aim is to provide delicious, satisfying recipes that are vegetarian and can be made easily, in minutes with a simple trip to Trader Joe's.

Why Trader Joe's?

We are always surprised when we run into someone who's never shopped at Trader Joe's, because we can't imagine life without it! Ask someone what they love most about Trader Joe's, and you'll likely hear some of these reasons:

- **Value and quality.** At Trader Joe's, you'll find everything from the very basics to high-end gourmet food at affordable prices. All the food is high quality and delicious, with organic and natural options found throughout the store.

- **Unique products.** Trader Joe's scouts the world for new and inspiring foods and beverages. Only those that pass Trader Joe's employee taste tests make it to stores.

- **Just food, no preservatives.** When you compare the labels on Trader Joe's products to items found at other stores, you'll notice something missing: a long list of chemicals, fillers, and preservatives.

- **No artificial flavors and no artificial colors.** Whether it's the "pink" in pink lemonade or the colorful candy coating on the Chocolate Sunflower Seed Drops, the colorings are natural (usually vegetable extracts) rather than synthetic food dyes. Flavorings are also natural, which not only taste better but are healthier.

- **Nothing genetically engineered.** Trader Joe's was among the first national grocers to remove genetically modified food from its private label products.

  - **Eco-conscious.** Trader Joe's is regularly recognized for its commitment to responsible buying practices. Trader Joe's brand eggs are cage-free. Hormone-free dairy products are the norm.

    - **Wine and beer.** In addition to great food, Trader Joe's brings a wide and ever-evolving assortment of value-priced wines from all over the globe, including the famously nicknamed "Two-Buck Chuck." Trader Joe's international beer selection is second to none.

      - **Fun-filled shopping experience.** Balloons, hand-written chalkboard signs, lively music, and cheerful crewmembers decked in Hawaiian flair create a friendly and casual atmosphere.

        - **Vegetarian and vegan product listing.** Take a look at Trader Joe's website and you'll see a pretty comprehensive list of vegetarian and vegan products available at the store.

          So head on down to your nearest Trader Joe's with this cookbook in hand, and let us show you why this is our favorite grocer and our favorite way to cook.

About our recipes and this book

The vegetarian recipes in this collection include:

1. Photos for every recipe.
We love cookbooks with photos. How else will you know if you'll like a recipe or what it will look like when it's done? We think it's necessary to have pictures with recipes, so we're continuing our tradition of giving you a photo of every single dish, made by us, in our own kitchens.

2. One-stop shopping at Trader Joe's.
We're too busy to run around from store to store, gathering ingredients. And we know you are, too. The recipes in this book are built on one-stop shopping: get everything you need at Trader Joe's and then get ready for the easiest cooking you can imagine. Throughout the book, we've capitalized the names of unique Trader Joe's products, such as Fresh Bruschetta Sauce or Chunky Salsa. Of course, it's not a *requirement* to get everything at Trader Joe's, but it's a convenience we invite you to embrace. And yes, we recognize that occasionally an item will be out of stock or (heaven forbid!) discontinued. That's why we suggest substitutions in recipes and keep a running list of substitutions on our website, **cookingwithtraderjoes.com.**

3. Nutritional information.
A team of certified dietitians and nutritionists has evaluated each recipe, and nutritional data is given so you can match menus to your dietary needs. Whether you're interested in carbs, calories, or fat, whether you follow popular diets or have your own regimen, we hope the nutritional data provided in this book will help you create healthy menus.

Nutritional analysis for recipes assumes 1% milk, low-fat yogurt, and low-sodium broth unless otherwise noted. It does not include optional ingredients.

Many cheeses are made with animal rennet. Some vegetarians eat cheese, some don't, and some seek out cheese made with vegetarian rennet. For the purposes of this book, we consider cheese to be vegetarian.

We note recipes that can be made gluten free using simple substitutions.

Apricot Baked Brie 13

Roasted Garlic (Friends Be Damned) 14

Homemade Hummus 16

Indian Spinach Pizza 17

Tomato and Mozzarella Skewers 19

Pisto Manchego 20

Olive-Stuffed Bread 23

Just Peachy Dip 24

Cheese & Chutney Mini-Rolls 25

California Caviar (Bean Salsa) 26

Ten-Layer Mexican Dip 28

Warm Honeyed Figs with Goat Cheese 31

Creamy Stuffed Mushroom Caps 32

Kickin' Artichoke Dip 35

Strawberry Mango Salsa 36

Appetizers

Apricot Baked Brie

When Deana was school age, her mom would order a prepared apricot Brie from the specialty grocery store in town, which only stocked it seasonally. She really didn't care for plain old Brie back then, but when that warm, apricot-covered melty concoction came out of the oven, she couldn't get enough. Even if you think you don't like Brie, try this baked version; you may not recognize it. This warm and creamy cheese dish is a great accompaniment to some grapes and a bottle of wine. One night, we had this dish with our Roasted Garlic (page 14) as appetizers and enjoyed it so much that we kept on eating and skipped dinner.

1 (~0.6 lb) wedge Brie cheese, such as Double Crème Brie
2 heaping Tbsp apricot preserves, such as Organic Reduced Sugar Apricot Preserves
1 handful raw sliced almonds
1 Tbsp Triple Sec (optional)
1 box water crackers

1 Preheat oven to 400° F.

2 Place the wedge of Brie in a small baking dish that is slightly bigger than the Brie. Top with apricot preserves, sprinkle on almonds, and drizzle Triple Sec over the top.

3 Cover tightly with foil and bake for 12-14 minutes or until cheese is melting. Remove from oven and serve with water crackers. Before your guests attack the Brie unrelentingly, remind them that the dish is hot.

Prep time: *5 minutes*
Hands-off cooking time: *12-14 minutes*
Serves *8*

Nutrition Snapshot
Per serving: 181 calories, 10 g fat, 6 g saturated fat, 9 g protein, 13 g carbs, 0 g fiber, 1 g sugar, 254 mg sodium

G
Gluten Free

*Use Savory Thins
rice crackers*

Roasted Garlic (Friends Be Damned)

Roasting mellows garlic's strong flavor, turning it into a creamy spread perfect for crackers or crusty bread. Our young kids eat it straight from the bulb. Pair with cheese, mix with mashed potatoes, or add to pasta dishes and steaks for great flavor. Garlic aids digestion and keeps your immune system strong. Garlic also contains allicin, a compound that reduces unhealthy fats and cholesterol in your body. Baking or roasting it whole (or eating it raw, of course, but that's between you and your friends) is the best way to preserve its many medicinal properties.

Whole bulbs of garlic
1 Tbsp extra virgin olive oil per bulb
Freshly ground black pepper

1   Preheat oven to 400° F.

2   With a knife, cut tops off garlic bulbs, slicing across tips of cloves. Place each bulb on a square of aluminum foil, drizzle with olive oil, and sprinkle with pepper.

3   Wrap foil around each bulb and toss the wrapped bulbs in the oven (straight on the rack) for 30-40 minutes or until garlic cloves are completely soft and beginning to caramelize. (Just open the foil and take a peek.) For a large bulb (2.5 inches across), cooking time will be about 40 minutes.

4   When you gently press at the base of the clove, it will easily squeeze out whole.

Prep time: *5 minutes*
Hands-off cooking time: *40 minutes*
A large bulb serves *4*

Nutrition Snapshot
Per serving: 36 calories, 4 g fat, 1 g saturated fat, 0 g protein, 1 g carbs, 0 g fiber, 0 g sugar, 2 mg sodium

Gluten Free

Homemade Hummus

Hummus is a thick, smooth spread made of mashed garbanzo beans (also called chickpeas or ceci beans), olive oil, lemon juice, garlic, and tahini, and it's very popular around the world. It's easy to find ready-made, but it's almost as easy to make your own fresh version. A few hours or even a day in the fridge enhances the taste by giving the flavors time to meld.

2 (15-oz) cans garbanzo beans
1 clove garlic, crushed, or 1 cube frozen Crushed Garlic
½ tsp cumin
¼ tsp salt
1 Tbsp sesame tahini
¼ cup extra virgin olive oil
2 Tbsp lemon juice (juice of 1 lemon)

1 Drain one of the cans of beans. Add both cans (including the juices of one can) to blender or food processor.

2 Add remaining ingredients and purée until hummus is smooth.

3 For best flavor, store in fridge for a few hours before serving.

Prep time: *10 minutes,* **Serves** *10*

Nutrition Snapshot
Per serving: 124 calories, 6 g fat, 1 g saturated fat, 4 g protein, 14 g carbs, 4 g fiber, 1 g sugar, 339 mg sodium

Tip: *When serving, garnish with pine nuts, a sprinkle of paprika, a drizzle of olive oil, or chopped parsley. Serve with pita chips, pita bread, vegetables, or in a wrap or falafel sandwich.*

Gluten Free

Indian Spinach Pizza

Tandoori Naan is an Indian flatbread that gets its name from the tandoor (clay oven) in which it is baked. Trader Joe's carries fresh and frozen tandoori naan in a few flavors. Keep a bag of the frozen tandoori naan in the fridge, and it will come in handy when cooking curry or making this easy ethnic-crossover appetizer.

2 pieces of frozen Tandoori Naan, plain

4 Tbsp Masala Simmer Sauce

1 cup frozen spinach, thawed and drained (squeeze water out with your hands)

2 Tbsp ricotta cheese

½ cup diced tomatoes

1 Preheat oven to 400° F.

2 Spread sauce on top of each naan.

3 Sprinkle on spinach and small pieces of ricotta.

4 Bake for 5 minutes.

5 Remove from oven and top with tomatoes.

Prep time: *5 minutes,* **Hands-off cooking time:** *5 minutes,* **Makes** *2 small pizzas*

Nutrition Snapshot
Per ½ pizza: 163 calories, 3 g fat, 1 g saturated fat, 6 g protein, 26 g carbs, 2 g fiber, 3 g sugar, 271 mg sodium

Tomato and Mozzarella Skewers

If you liked the Caprese Salad in our original cookbook, *Cooking with All Things Trader Joe's* (page 34), you'll love this party-ready version. We've kabobbed the classic Caprese ingredients – tomatoes, mozzarella, and basil – to create an easy and festive appetizer with all the colors of red, white, and skew. Who says finger food can't be classy?

1 (8-oz) container Ciliegine fresh mozzarella balls
1 (8-oz) pkg cherry tomatoes or grape tomatoes
1 bunch fresh basil leaves
1 Tbsp olive oil
Pinch salt
Pinch black pepper
Wooden skewers

1 Thread one mozzarella ball, one tomato, and one small basil leaf onto each skewer.

2 Drizzle with olive oil. Sprinkle with sea salt and freshly ground black pepper.

Prep time: *15 minutes*
Makes *24 skewers*

Nutrition Snapshot
Per skewer: 27 calories, 2 g fat, 1 g saturated fat, 2 g protein, 0.4 g carbs, 0.1 g fiber, 0.2 g sugar, 25 mg sodium

Tip: *For more flavor, use garlic-infused olive oil. You can make your own by slowly heating olive oil and sliced garlic in a pan. When edges of garlic start to brown, remove from heat. Let cool to room temperature, and discard garlic slices.*

Gluten Free

Pisto Manchego

Pisto Manchego is best described as a puréed Spanish ratatouille, typically made with a combination of eggplant, zucchini, red bell pepper, garlic, and olive oil. We make it in a snap using Trader Joe's Misto Alla Griglia (frozen Marinated Grilled Eggplant & Zucchini) and jarred roasted red peppers. It's absolutely delicious served with crusty bread, pita chips, or cut veggies. Pisto Manchego is also commonly served in Spain as an entrée, with the texture left more chunky than puréed, and topped with a fried egg.

1 (16-oz) bag frozen Misto Alla Griglia, thawed
2 (12-oz) jars Fire Roasted Red Peppers, drained
2 cloves garlic, crushed, or 2 cubes frozen Crushed Garlic
Pinch cumin
½ tsp dried oregano

1   In a food processor, blend together all ingredients until smooth.

Prep time: *5 minutes*
Serves *8*

Nutrition Snapshot
Per serving: 80 calories, 5g fat, 1g saturated fat, 1g protein, 7g carbs, 4g fiber, 3g sugar, 235mg sodium

Gluten Free

Olive-Stuffed Bread

A few minutes of work yields a rustic yet sophisticated crusty herbed-bread loaf with the salty surprise of olives inside. It's a nice bread to enjoy warm with cheese and an appetizer, or with a full meal.

1 (1-lb) bag refrigerated pizza dough
½ cup Green Olive Tapenade or your favorite bruschetta or tapenade

1 Preheat oven to 425° F.

2 On a floured surface, roll dough (or stretch out with hands) so it is about 6 x 15 inches. Spoon tapenade down the center lengthwise, except for the last inch at each end. Pull up sides of bread and firmly pinch a seam down the center, sealing in tapenade.

3 Place seam-side down on a pizza stone (preferred method) or an oiled baking sheet and bake for 30-35 minutes, or until crust is golden brown.

4 Slice loaf into 1-inch pieces and serve warm.

Prep time: *5 minutes*
Hands-off cooking time: *30 minutes*
Serves *8*

Nutrition Snapshot
Per serving: 150 calories, 4 g fat, 0 g saturated fat, 3 g protein, 25 g carbs, 1 g fiber, 0 g sugar, 660 mg sodium

Just Peachy Dip

Enjoy this simple mix-and-serve dip at your next party. Whipped cream cheese and spicy peach salsa are transformed into a creamy dip – perfect with pita chips, tortilla chips, or veggies. This salsa is mild; for a little more kick, choose a spicier salsa.

½ cup Spicy Smoky Peach Salsa
4 oz light whipped cream cheese

1   Mix salsa and cream cheese in a small bowl until smooth.

Prep time: *5 minutes*
Serves *8*

Nutrition Snapshot

Per serving: 36 calories, 2 g fat, 1 g saturated fat, 1 g protein, 3 g carbs, 0 g fiber, 3 g sugar, 111 mg sodium

G
Gluten Free

Cheese & Chutney Mini-Rolls

We commend the British for coming up with the great pairing of cheddar and chutney. In fact, any hard or semi-hard cheese would be superb here, such as Parmesan, Gruyère, or Stilton. These rolls can be made ahead of time and kept covered in the fridge. If miniature buns are not available, make tea sandwiches using sandwich bread.

1 (7-oz) pkg Mini Hamburger Buns (8 buns)
4 oz aged sharp cheddar or Cave Aged Gruyere, sliced into 8 pieces
4 Tbsp Mango Ginger Chutney

1   Make each sandwich with a slice of cheese and spoonful of chutney.

Prep time: *5 minutes*
Serves *8 (1 roll per serving)*

Nutrition Snapshot
Per serving (1 roll): 151 calories, 6 g fat, 3 g saturated fat, 5 g protein, 19 g carbs, 1 g fiber, 5 g sugar, 107 mg sodium

Gluten Free

Substitute gluten-free bread for the buns and make tea sandwiches, or serve cheese and chutney on Savory Thins rice crackers.

California Caviar (Bean Salsa)

California Caviar is our West Coast interpretation of Texas Caviar, the classic bean salsa traditionally eaten with tortilla chips. Texas Caviar is usually made with smoky black eyed peas, but we use black beans and edamame. Creamy diced avocado and flavorful Corn and Chile Tomato-less Salsa add texture and a sweet-spicy punch of flavor

1 (15-oz) can black beans, rinsed and drained
1 (9-oz) pkg shelled edamame (2 cups)
1 (13.75-oz) jar Corn and Chile Tomato-less Salsa
1 ripe avocado, diced

1 Stir together all ingredients in a medium serving bowl or platter.

Prep time: *5 minutes*
Serves *8*

Nutrition Snapshot

Per serving: 161 calories, 3g fat, 1g saturated fat, 8g protein, 26g carbs, 5g fiber, 9g sugar, 365mg sodium

Gluten Free

Ten-Layer Mexican Dip

It may seem complex at first glance, but this delicious layered dip comes together in minutes by combining convenience items with fresh ingredients. This recipe makes a big party batch and can be customized with your favorite ingredients. To make a heartier dish, substitute a can of chili for the refried beans. Enjoy with tortilla chips or pita chips.

1 (16-oz) can Fat Free Refried Beans, Refried Pinto Beans, or Refried Black Beans with Jalapeño
1 (8-oz) tray Avocado's Number Guacamole, or your favorite guacamole
8 oz (½ a container) light or regular sour cream
1 cup salsa, such as Double Roasted Salsa or Chunky Salsa
1 cup shredded lettuce
1 cup chopped tomatoes
⅓ cup sliced black olives, drained
2 green onions, chopped
2 Tbsp chopped fresh cilantro
1 cup Fancy Shredded Mexican Cheese Blend

1 Choose a glass dish, approximately 8 x 8-inches.

2 Spread refried beans on bottom of dish and continue layering with guacamole, sour cream, and salsa. If guacamole or sour cream is difficult to spread, add dollops over the previous layer. Sprinkle on lettuce, tomato, olives, green onions, cilantro and cheese.

Variation: *For an extra spicy kick, mix ½ tsp Taco Seasoning into sour cream.*

Prep time: *10 minutes*
Serves *12*

Nutrition Snapshot
Per serving: 136 calories, 9 g fat, 3 g saturated fat, 5 g protein, 10 g carbs, 3 g fiber, 3 g sugar, 469 mg sodium

Gluten Free

Warm Honeyed Figs with Goat Cheese

When figs are in season, enjoy the classic combination of sweet ripe figs and tangy goat cheese as an appetizer or even as dessert. Fresh figs spoil quickly, so plan on using them within a day or so.

12 medium or large fresh figs
1 tsp extra virgin olive oil
1 Tbsp honey
2 oz goat cheese

1   Cut each fig in half, from stem to end.

2   Heat olive oil in a skillet over medium heat. Place figs in skillet cut side down and sauté for 1-2 minutes until faces are hot and slightly caramelized. Remove from heat.

3   Drizzle figs with honey and gently toss to distribute honey.

4   Place figs face up on a platter. Place a few crumbles of goat cheese in the center of each fig. Goat cheese will soften slightly from the heat of the figs. Serve immediately.

Variation: *Substitute mascarpone for goat cheese.*

Prep and cooking time: *10 minutes*
Serves *6 (4 pieces per serving)*

Nutrition Snapshot
Per serving: 146 calories, 4 g fat, 2 g saturated fat, 3 g protein, 28 g carbs, 4 g fiber, 24 g sugar, 35 mg sodium

Note: *If using very small figs, cut off tops, slice down into tops just a little, sauté, and stuff with goat cheese.*

Creamy Stuffed Mushroom Caps

Everyone loves stuffed mushrooms, and the creamy filling makes these bite-size morsels especially satisfying. For the filling, we combine spinach with Boursin, an herbed cheese spread (look for it boxed in white cardboard packaging). To create a side dish, use larger stuffing mushrooms or stuffing Portabellas.

40 regular mushrooms or 18 stuffing mushrooms or small Portabellas, cleaned and stems removed
1 (5.2-oz) container Boursin Garlic & Fine Herbs Gournay Cheese
3 cups (½ a 16-oz bag) frozen spinach, thawed
¼ cup bread crumbs

1   Preheat oven to 350° F.

2   Drain thawed spinach, squeezing out water firmly with hands. 3 cups frozen spinach should reduce to ½ cup thawed after water has been squeezed out.

3   Combine Boursin and spinach in a small bowl.

4   Stuff mushroom caps with spinach mixture.

5   Spread bread crumbs on a plate. Take each mushroom and press, spinach side down, into bread crumbs, coating fully. Arrange caps on baking sheet or dish, stuffing side up.

6   Bake 12-15 minutes until water starts to appear under caps. Do not overcook.

Prep time: *10 minutes*
Hands-off cooking time: *15 minutes*
Serves *10 (2 mushrooms per serving)*

Nutrition Snapshot
Per serving: 104 calories, 8 g fat, 4 g saturated fat, 4 g protein, 8 g carbs, 0 g fiber, 4 g sugar, 148 mg sodium

Substitute almond meal for bread crumbs

Kickin' Artichoke Dip

Marcy Cascone from San Juan Capistrano, California, won one of our recipe contests with this entry. Trader Joe's sells ready-made artichoke dips, but we think this one is even better, and it takes only a few minutes of prep. The star of the recipe is the sweet and spicy pecan topping that contrasts beautifully with the dip. Serve with pita chips, tortilla chips, or Savory Thins rice crackers.

1 (12-oz) jar Marinated Artichoke Hearts, drained and chopped
1 cup reduced-fat or regular mayonnaise
1 cup shredded Parmesan cheese
1 (8-oz) pkg light or regular cream cheese, softened
1 (5-oz) bag Sweet & Spicy Pecans, chopped

1   Preheat oven to 350° F.

2   Mix all ingredients together except nuts.

3   Transfer mixture to a small baking dish and spread to flatten. Sprinkle chopped pecans on top.

4   Bake for 35 minutes, or until dip is heated through and edges are bubbly. Drape with foil if pecans begin to brown too much. Serve immediately.

Variation: *If you can't bear to part with Trader Joe's ready-made Grilled Artichoke & Parmesan Dip, borrow the topping from this recipe for a tasty twist. Buy two containers of dip and empty into an oven safe dish. Sprinkle chopped Sweet & Spicy Pecans on top and bake per recipe.*

Prep time: *10 minutes*
Hands-off cooking time: *35 minutes*
Serves *32 (2 Tbsp per serving)*

Nutrition Snapshot
Per serving: 89 calories, 7 g fat, 2 g saturated fat, 2 g protein, 3 g carbs, 1 g fiber, 2 g sugar, 172 mg sodium

Gluten Free

Strawberry Mango Salsa

When ripe strawberries and juicy mango are in season, let them shine in a fruit salsa with just a hint of lime. A fruit salsa is a miniature version of a fruit salad – the very small dice makes it a condiment you can pick up with chips or enjoy on other foods. Serve with cinnamon pita chips for a real flavor surprise or with regular pita chips for a more subdued palate. Don't throw away leftovers! Toss them in a blender with yogurt and ice for a terrific smoothie.

2 cups finely diced strawberries
2 cups finely diced mango
2 Tbsp fresh lime or lemon juice
¼ cup chopped mint or cilantro (optional)

1   Stir all ingredients gently in a serving bowl.

2   Allow to rest for 15 minutes for flavors to meld.

Prep time: *15 minutes*
Serves: *8*

Nutrition Snapshot

Per serving: 41 calories, 0 g fat, 0 g saturated fat, 1 g protein, 11 g carbs, 2 g fiber, 8 g sugar, 1 mg sodium

G
Gluten Free

Note: *Trader Joe's usually sells containers of peeled and cut mango, a convenient shortcut to enjoying this fruit.*

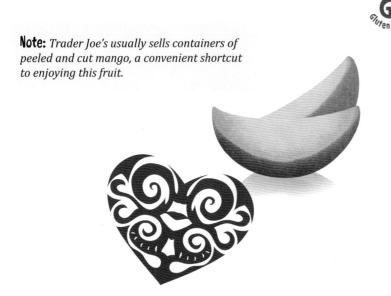

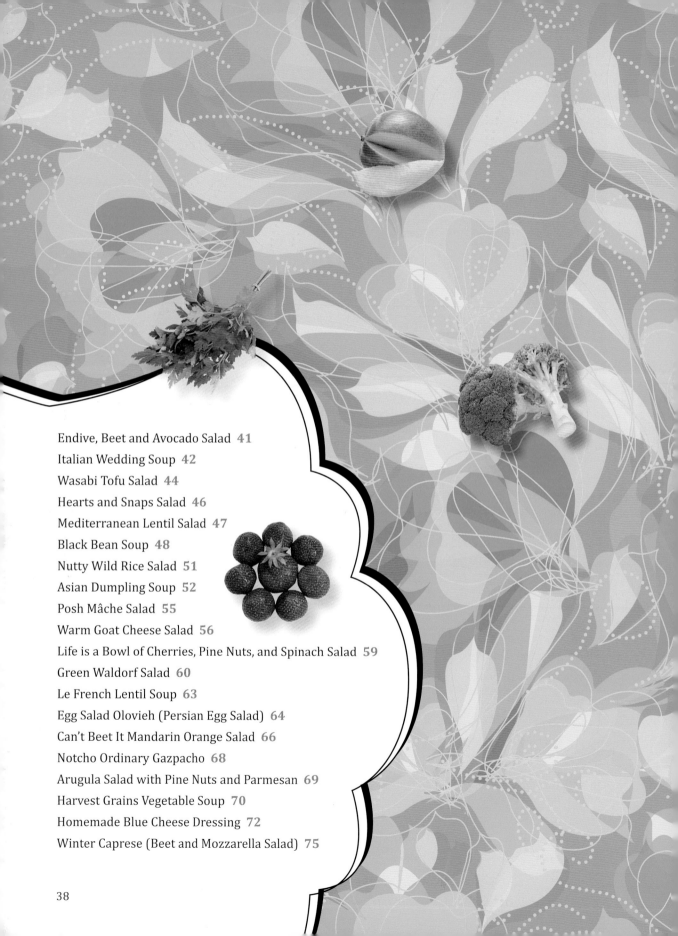

Endive, Beet and Avocado Salad 41

Italian Wedding Soup 42

Wasabi Tofu Salad 44

Hearts and Snaps Salad 46

Mediterranean Lentil Salad 47

Black Bean Soup 48

Nutty Wild Rice Salad 51

Asian Dumpling Soup 52

Posh Mâche Salad 55

Warm Goat Cheese Salad 56

Life is a Bowl of Cherries, Pine Nuts, and Spinach Salad 59

Green Waldorf Salad 60

Le French Lentil Soup 63

Egg Salad Olovieh (Persian Egg Salad) 64

Can't Beet It Mandarin Orange Salad 66

Notcho Ordinary Gazpacho 68

Arugula Salad with Pine Nuts and Parmesan 69

Harvest Grains Vegetable Soup 70

Homemade Blue Cheese Dressing 72

Winter Caprese (Beet and Mozzarella Salad) 75

Soups & Salads

Endive, Beet, and Avocado Salad

Crunchy endive, colorful beets, and ripe avocado chunks are married with a light citrus vinaigrette. The sweetness of the beets and creaminess of the avocado perfectly balance the slightly bitter taste of endive. Ready-to-eat boiled and peeled baby beets take the work out of this fantastic salad.

1 pkg Red and White Belgian Endive (3 small heads endive), sliced
1 (8-oz) pkg Steamed and Peeled Baby Beets, chopped into ½-inch pieces
1 ripe avocado, cubed
¼ cup Crumbled Goat Cheese

Citrus Dressing
2 Tbsp extra virgin olive oil
2 Tbsp orange juice
1 tsp fresh thyme

1   Whisk together dressing ingredients. Toss endive with dressing until well coated.

2   Add beets and avocado and give a gentle toss. Sprinkle goat cheese on top.

Prep Time: *10 minutes*
Serves *4*

Nutrition Snapshot
Per serving: 182 calories, 9 g fat, 1 g saturated fat, 16 g protein, 13 g carbs, 5 g fiber, 4 g sugar, 671 mg sodium

G
Gluten Free

Italian Wedding Soup

Despite common belief, the name for this soup actually has nothing to do with a couple's big day. In Italian, two things that go well together are said to be "well married," and the country has long enjoyed this soup's winning combination of greens and meat (or in this case, vegetarian meatballs).

1 (16 oz) bag frozen Meatless Meatballs

1 Tbsp extra virgin olive oil

1 small onion, chopped, or 1 cup bagged Freshly Diced Onions

1 clove garlic, crushed, or 1 cube frozen Crushed Garlic

½ cup diced carrots or halved baby carrots

4 cups (one 32-oz carton) low-sodium vegetable broth

3 cups Swiss chard or spinach (if using frozen spinach, use only 1 cup)

¼ cup chopped fresh parsley

¼ cup grated or shredded Parmesan cheese

1   Heat olive oil over medium-high heat. Add onions, garlic, and carrots. Cook for 5 minutes.

2   Add broth and meatballs. Bring mixture to a boil. Reduce heat and simmer for 20 minutes. Add Swiss chard and boil for 5 minutes longer.

3   Ladle into soup bowls. Garnish with parsley and Parmesan cheese.

Prep time: *15 minutes*
Hands-off cooking time: *20 minutes*
Serves 6

Nutrition Snapshot
Per serving: 179 calories, 11 g fat, 4 g saturated fat, 11 g protein, 8 g carbs, 1 g fiber, 2 g sugar, 402 mg sodium

Wasabi Tofu Salad

Tofu isn't boring when it's penetrated with intense flavors of soy, garlic, ginger, and sesame oil. Contrast the marinated tofu with the fresh crunch of vegetables and crisp lettuce. Swap lettuce with shredded cabbage for a salad that can last an extra day in the fridge. Addictive wasabi peas add crunch, spice, and an eye-watering kick!

1 (19-oz) pkg regular or firm tofu

⅓ cup Soyaki or Sesame Soy Ginger Vinaigrette

2 tsp toasted sesame oil

1 Tbsp apple cider vinegar

1 (5-oz) bag Baby Spring Mix, or equivalent amount of any salad greens

3 Persian cucumbers

2 green onions

1 box (pint) cherry tomatoes

½ cup Wasabi Peas

1 Dice tofu into ½-inch pieces. Place in a small bowl.

2 For the dressing, mix together Soyaki, sesame oil, and vinegar.

3 Drain excess liquid from diced tofu, then pour dressing over tofu and let marinate for 10 minutes while you prepare remaining ingredients.

4 Chop cucumbers (no need to peel) and slice green onions. Place lettuce, cucumbers, green onions, and tomatoes in a large bowl.

5 Pour tofu and dressing over salad. Toss gently to combine. When serving, top with a sprinkle of wasabi peas for added punch.

Prep time: *15 minutes*
Serves *4*

Nutrition Snapshot

Per serving: 250 calories, 12 g fat, 1 g saturated fat, 15 g protein, 23 g carbs, 4 g fiber, 11 g sugar, 692 mg sodium

Substitute tamari or wheat-free soy sauce for the Soyaki and substitute cashews for the wasabi peas

Hearts and Snaps Salad

Hearts of palm are great straight out of the can and are high in iron and vitamins (and low in calories). Combine them with sweet snap peas, refreshing cucumber, ripe tomatoes, tangy feta, and fresh parsley for a cool and quick salad. This crispy, fresh dish can be used as a colorful starter salad or light side dish. A splash of creamy dressing brings it all together.

1 cup sliced hearts of palm (about 3 sticks), available canned or fresh
1 cup chopped cucumbers (about 2 Persian cucumbers or 1 medium cucumber)
1 cup halved or quartered cherry/cocktail tomatoes
1 cup sugar snap peas, chopped in thirds
¼ cup chopped parsley (cilantro may be substituted)
¼ cup Crumbled Feta
¼ cup Goddess Dressing

1   Combine vegetables, cheese, and parsley in a bowl.

2   Toss with dressing.

Prep time: *10 minutes*
Serves *4*

Nutrition Snapshot
Per serving: 138 calories, 9 g fat, 1 g saturated fat, 5 g protein, 10 g carbs, 3 g fiber, 5 g sugar, 276 mg sodium

Gluten Free

Mediterranean Lentil Salad

Tender pre-cooked lentils make this salad a mix-and-serve breeze. The light, lemony, fresh taste makes it a great side dish or light lunch. Serve with our Olive-Stuffed Bread (page 23). If you have leftovers, improvise a little and use them in our Hummus and Lentil Wrap (page 145).

1 (17.6-oz) pkg refrigerated Steamed Lentils (about 2 ½ cups)
1 ½ cups chopped tomato (we like to use cocktail tomatoes or baby Romas in this recipe)
½ cup chopped fresh parsley
1 Tbsp fresh mint (optional)
1 Tbsp lemon juice
2 Tbsp extra virgin olive oill

1   Combine lentils, tomatoes, parsley, and mint.

2   Whisk together lemon juice and olive oil. Pour dressing over salad, stirring gently to combine.

Prep time: *5 minutes*
Serves *6*

Nutrition Snapshot
Per serving: 227 calories, 7 g fat, 1 g saturated fat, 14 g protein, 29 g carbs, 11 g fiber, 4 g sugar, 308 mg sodium

Black Bean Soup

One of our favorites. This soup is hearty and spicy, thanks to the warm earthy flavor of cumin and the zing of fresh lime. We like it with tortilla chips on the side. It makes a great meal by itself, or it can be paired with one of our quesadilla recipes for a bigger meal. Black beans are not only high in fiber and folate, they also rival grapes and cranberries for their antioxidant properties. Sensitive to sulfites? Black beans contain the trace mineral molybdenum, which counteracts sulfites. So uncork that bottle of red later tonight.

1 medium yellow onion, peeled and chopped, or 1 ½ cups bagged Freshly Diced Onions

1 clove garlic, crushed, or 1 cube frozen Crushed Garlic

2 Tbsp extra virgin olive oil

1 tsp ground cumin

2 (15-oz) cans black beans (do not drain)

1 cup (half a jar) Chunky Salsa

2 Tbsp lime juice (juice of 1 lime)

Plain yogurt, such as Plain Cream Line Yogurt, or sour cream (optional)

1 In a medium pot, sauté onions in olive oil until they are soft and translucent.

2 Sprinkle in cumin and garlic and sauté for a minute; pour in black beans (including juices), salsa, and lime. Stir to combine and bring to a simmer. Simmer covered for 20 minutes.

3 Ladle soup into individual bowls and top with a dollop of yogurt.

Prep time: *10 minutes*
Hands-off cooking time: *20 minutes*
Serves *5*

Nutrition Snapshot
Per serving: 234 calories, 6 g fat, 1 g saturated fat, 9 g protein, 35 g carbs, 9 g fiber, 7 g sugar, 879 mg sodium

Gluten Free

48

Nutty Wild Rice Salad

Wild rice has a wonderful nutty flavor and hearty texture, making it perfect for salads, stuffing, pilaf, and soups. This entrée salad offers a symphony of textures: the chewiness of wild rice, the sweet burst of grapes, the crunch of cashews, and the crisp bite of green onion.

4 cups cooked wild rice, warm or cold

1 (9-oz) pkg shelled edamame (2 cups)

1 ½ cups red grapes, halved

1 cup roasted unsalted cashews, whole or pieces

3 stalks green onion, chopped

Citrus Vinaigrette

3 Tbsp extra virgin olive oil

1 Tbsp lemon juice

1 Tbsp white balsamic vinegar

1 Tbsp honey

1 clove garlic, crushed, or 1 cube frozen Crushed Garlic, thawed

⅛ tsp salt, or more to taste

1 In a large bowl, combine wild rice, edamame, grapes, cashews, and green onion.

2 In a small bowl, whisk together dressing ingredients. Pour over salad and stir to distribute evenly.

Prep time: *10 minutes (+ 45 minutes cooking time if not using pre-cooked rice)*
Serves *4*

Nutrition Snapshot
Per serving: 544 calories, 28g fat, 5g saturated fat, 18g protein, 59g carbs, 9g fiber, 17g sugar, 396mg sodium

Helpful Tip: *1 cup uncooked wild rice yields approximately 4 cups cooked wild rice.*

Asian Dumpling Soup

Here is our version of wonton soup using Asian steam-fried dumplings. In Japan, the dumplings are called *gyozas*, and in China, they are called *guo tie* (literally meaning "pot stick"), commonly known as potstickers. Most people are familiar with the pan-fried version served as an appetizer, but the dumplings also work well in soups. Adding a beaten egg at the end creates delicate ribbons reminiscent of egg drop soup.

1 (16-oz) bag frozen vegetarian gyoza or potstickers

4 cups (one 32-oz carton) vegetable broth

1 tsp soy sauce

1 clove garlic, crushed, or 1 cube frozen Crushed Garlic

3 cups refrigerated Stir Fry Vegetables, any variety, or frozen Stir-Fry Vegetables

1 egg (optional)

1 tsp toasted sesame oil

Black pepper to taste

1 In a medium pot, heat broth, soy sauce, and garlic over medium-high heat. Bring mixture to a boil. Add gyoza and vegetables. When mixture boils again, reduce heat to medium-low and cook for 5 minutes.

2 If using egg, beat with a fork until frothy. Slowly pour into boiling soup in a thin stream, creating cooked ribbons of egg. If you prefer, you can pan-fry the egg and cut into strips or squares. Use as a garnish.

3 Remove from heat. Stir in sesame oil. Sprinkle with black pepper to taste.

Prep and cooking time: *15 minutes*
Serves *4*

Nutrition Snapshot
Per serving: 239 calories, 4 g fat, 1 g saturated fat, 9 g protein, 39 g carbs, 7 g fiber, 12 g sugar, 843 mg sodium

Warm Goat Cheese Salad

Goat cheese rounds are heated just enough to create a crusty layer without melting the cheese. This restaurant favorite is easy to make at home, especially with pre-sliced goat cheese medallions. We use almond meal instead of traditional bread crumbs, both for flavor and nutritional value.

1 (5.4-oz) pkg Chevre Medallions or 1 (8-oz) log Chevre goat cheese, sliced

1 egg white, beaten

2 cups almond meal

2 Tbsp olive oil

1 (5-oz) bag Organics Baby Spring Mix salad

⅓ cup refrigerated Champagne Pear Vinaigrette or or your favorite dressing

1 Dip each goat cheese round in egg white and then coat in almond meal. If you're prepping ahead of time, place breaded goat cheese rounds in refrigerator until ready to cook. Cheese rounds should be cold and firm so they don't melt when fried.

2 Heat olive oil in a nonstick pan over medium heat. Fry cheese rounds for 1 minute on each side or until browned. Promptly remove from heat before cheese melts.

3 Pour vinaigrette over salad mix and toss until coated. Place warm cheese on dressed salad and serve immediately.

Prep and cooking time: *20 minutes*
Serves *4*

Nutrition Snapshot
Per serving: 392 calories, 29 g fat, 15 g saturated fat, 20 g protein, 13 g carbs, 1 g fiber, 5 g sugar, 376 mg sodium

G
Gluten Free

Tip: *If you're slicing a goat cheese log yourself, don't use a knife or you'll end up with a gooey mess. Using unflavored dental floss, hold both ends tightly and press taut floss down through goat cheese.*

Posh Mâche Salad

Mâche (pronounced "mosh"), also known as lamb's lettuce, is a delicate, buttery-textured lettuce with small rounded leaves. Toss with a mild dressing, such as our lemon vinaigrette below, to enjoy its subtle flavors. To complete this salad, we add fresh fruits and Trader Joe's addictive sesame honey coated cashews.

1 (4-oz) bag mâche
2 kiwi, peeled and sliced
1 cup sliced strawberries
½ cup Sesame Honey Cashews

Lemon Vinaigrette
3 Tbsp extra virgin olive oil
1 Tbsp lemon juice
1 tsp honey
Pinch salt and black pepper

1 In a salad bowl, combine mache, kiwi, strawberries, and cashews.

2 Whisk the dressing ingredients until emulsified and pour over salad, giving a toss to coat.

Prep time: *10 minutes*
Serves *4*

Nutrition Snapshot
Per serving: 213 calories, 16 g fat, 2 g saturated fat, 3 g protein, 16 g carbs, 2 g fiber, 48 mg sodium

Gluten Free

Life is a Bowl of Cherries, Pine Nuts, and Spinach Salad

The creation of this salad was a complete accident. Deana was at a potluck pottery workshop where she tried a tasty salad and asked the person who made it for the recipe. When she met the woman again, she thanked her for the recipe and told her that the pine nuts, cherries, and feta were amazing with the spinach. She laughed and said her salad recipe was arugula with blue cheese, walnuts, and apples. So much for memory... we still need to try her version. Montmorency cherries are the most popular sour cherry in the U.S., and they give a great sweet yet tart balance to the feta and pine nuts in this spinach salad. This salad is high in antioxidants from the cherries and in folic acid from the spinach (highest when raw).

1 (6-oz) bag baby spinach
½ cup Crumbled Feta cheese
½ cup dried Tart Montmorency Cherries

½ cup toasted pine nuts
6 Tbsp Balsamic Vinaigrette, or make your own (recipe below)

1 Combine ingredients, toss, and serve immediately.

2 The salad can be assembled ahead of time, but don't add the vinaigrette until you're ready to serve, or the spinach will wilt down.

Prep time: *5 minutes*
Serves *4*

Homemade Balsamic Vinaigrette

4 Tbsp extra virgin olive oil
2 Tbsp balsamic vinegar
¼ tsp dried basil

¼ tsp Dijon mustard
¼ tsp honey or a pinch of sugar

1 Whisk together vinaigrette ingredients.

2 Vinaigrette keeps for a few days in a closed container, such as a glass jar with a lid.

Nutrition Snapshot
Per serving: 249 calories, 22 g fat, 4 g saturated fat,
3 g protein, 14 g carbs, 2 g fiber, 9 g sugar, 151 mg sodium

Gluten Free

Green Waldorf Salad

This famous salad was invented at the Waldorf Astoria Hotel in New York City and has since appeared at countless holiday gatherings and buffet spreads. The original recipe calls for red apples, celery, and mayonnaise – and nothing else. We opt for tart flavors and lively green colors, while preserving the crunchiness and juiciness of the classic.

2 Granny Smith apples, diced
2 cups green grapes, halved
½ cup slivered almonds
¼ cup plain yogurt
1 Tbsp honey or agave nectar
¼ tsp salt
¼ tsp black pepper

1   Whisk yogurt, honey, salt, and pepper in a large bowl.

2   Stir in apples, grapes, and almonds. Toss lightly to coat.

3   Keep in fridge until ready to serve.

Prep time: *15 minutes*
Serves: *6*

Nutrition Snapshot
Per serving: 114 calories, 5 g fat, 0 g saturated fat, 3 g protein, 17 g carbs, 3 g fiber, 14 g sugar, 97 mg sodium

Gluten Free

Le French Lentil Soup

The best, most delicate lentils are French lentils, but they take longer to cook than other varieties. Thanks to Trader Joe's imported pre-cooked lentils, this earthy soup can be made in minutes instead of hours. This recipe has fooled guests who staunchly claimed to dislike lentils, so test it on your own lentil-phobe.

1 (17.6-oz) pkg refrigerated Steamed Lentils (about 2 ½ cups)
2 Tbsp olive oil
1 large onion, chopped, or 2 cups bagged Freshly Diced Onions
1 potato, peeled and diced (about 1 cup)
1 cup sliced carrots
1 tsp ground cumin
4 cups (one 32-oz carton) vegetable broth or water
1 Tbsp fresh lemon juice
Salt and pepper to taste
2 Tbsp chopped cilantro
Sour cream (optional)

1   Heat olive oil in a large saucepan over medium-high heat.

2   Cook onions, potatoes, and carrots for 10 minutes or until onions soften. Stir in cumin; cook for 1 minute longer to toast cumin.

3   Add broth and lentils. Bring to a boil and cook for 5-10 minutes longer, or until potatoes are cooked.

4   Remove from heat and stir in lemon juice. Add salt and pepper to taste.

5   Garnish with sour cream and cilantro.

Prep and cooking time: *20-30 minutes*
Serves *6*

Nutrition Snapshot
Per serving: 173 calories, 5 g fat, 1 g saturated fat, 9 g protein, 24 g carbs, 8 g fiber, 6 g sugar, 475 mg sodium

Use gluten-free broth

Egg Salad Olovieh (Persian Egg Salad)

Salad Olovieh is a Persian (also Russian) egg and potato salad complemented by pickles, peas, olives, olive oil, mayonnaise, and lemon. As far as egg salad goes, it's simply the best around. It's a great dish to make for large gatherings and goes over well with kids.

12 eggs
4 large Russet potatoes (about 4 cups total after cooked)
2 cups frozen peas
1 cup chopped dill pickles
½ cup sliced kalamata or black olives
¾ cup mayonnaise
3 Tbsp extra virgin olive oil
2 Tbsp fresh lemon juice
Salt and pepper to taste

1   Boil potatoes (unpeeled) in a pot of water with the water 1 inch above top of potatoes. Boil for 45 minutes or until potatoes are soft when poked with a knife. Drain. Boiled potatoes peel very easily – just use your fingers to slip skin off.

2   While potatoes are cooking, boil eggs. Fill pot with cold water, add eggs gently, and place over high heat. When water comes to a boil, remove pot from heat, cover, and let it sit for 15 minutes. Drain, run under cold water, and peel.

3   Mash potatoes in a large bowl (coarsely, don't try to get it very smooth), and add frozen peas while potatoes are still hot. The heat will thaw the peas.

4   Roughly chop eggs. To the potatoes, add eggs, pickles, and olives and combine.

5   Add mayo, olive oil, and lemon juice to the mixture, stirring until mayo is evenly distributed throughout. Add salt and pepper to taste.

6   Chill in fridge and serve with pita pockets, baguette pieces, or other favorite sandwich bread.

Prep time: *About 45 minutes of boiling (eggs and potatoes), but only 10 minutes of prep time after that*
Serves *12*

Nutrition Snapshot
Per serving: 326 calories, 16 g fat, 3 g saturated fat, 17 g protein, 30 g carbs, 3 g fiber, 4 g sugar, 384 mg sodium

Tip: *What makes some hard boiled eggs easy to peel when other times you need a hammer and chisel? For eggs that peel easily, let them stay in your fridge for 4 or 5 days first before hard boiling. Very fresh eggs are hard to peel when hard boiled.*

Gluten Free

Can't Beet It Mandarin Orange Salad

This colorful salad combines the fresh flavors and colors of fall. Forget the days of cooking and peeling your own beets, and say goodbye to clothes stained with beet juice. Fully prepared beets are at your beck and call in the produce section. To save time, we use canned Mandarin oranges, but fresh orange, grapefruit, or Clementine tangerine segments would also be good.

1 (8-oz) pkg refrigerated Steamed & Peeled Baby Beets (about 5 small beets)

3 Tbsp refrigerated Champagne Pear Vinaigrette or Homemade Orange Champagne Vinaigrette (recipe below)

1 (11-oz) can Mandarin oranges, drained

1 Tbsp chopped fresh mint or basil

1 Tbsp Crumbled Goat Cheese

1   Cut beets into quarters. Pour vinaigrette over beets and stir.

2   Add orange segments and toss very gently; the orange segments are fragile.

3   Sprinkle mint and goat cheese crumbles on top.

Homemade Orange Champagne Vinaigrette

½ tsp Hot & Sweet Mustard, or ¼ tsp mustard + ¼ tsp honey

1 Tbsp Orange Muscat Champagne Vinegar

2 Tbsp extra virgin olive oil

Generous pinch of salt

1   Whisk all ingredients together until dressing becomes a creamy emulsion.

Prep time: *10 minutes*

Serves *4*

Nutrition Snapshot

Per serving: 146 calories, 8 g fat,
1 g saturated fat, 1 g protein,
18 g carbs, 1 g fiber, 16 g sugar,
114 mg sodium

G
Gluten Free

Notcho Ordinary Gazpacho

Our take on the famous cold Andalusian soup, fresh with the aroma and cooling taste of cucumber and cilantro. A light and refreshing soup for a summer meal served on the patio. Don't forget the sangria!

4 cups (one 32-oz carton) Organic Creamy Tomato Soup

2 cups peeled and coarsely chopped cucumber (2 medium-sized cucumbers)

3 Tbsp lime juice (juice of 2 limes)

1 green bell pepper, stems and seeds removed

1 cup Soup & Oyster Crackers

1 cup Chunky Salsa

2 Tbsp cilantro

1   Combine all ingredients in a blender, saving a bit of cilantro or a few cucumber slices for garnish.

2   Pureé until smooth. Chill and serve cold.

Prep time: *15 minutes*, **Serves** *4*

Nutrition Snapshot
Per serving: 160 calories, 6 g fat, 2 g saturated fat, 2 g protein, 26 g carbs, 3 g fiber, 6 g sugar, 42 mg sodium

Arugula Salad with Pine Nuts and Parmesan

This recipe is courtesy of Uncle Bill, a wine connoisseur, restaurateur, and food expert. This salad is perfect in its simplicity. Measurements aren't necessary – if you love pine nuts, add more pine nuts. If you love Parmesan, load it on. If you want to make a light meal, boil some pasta (half a bag of penne) and toss it all together, allowing the arugula to wilt slightly.

1 (7-oz) bag arugula leaves (about 5 cups)
¼ cup extra virgin olive oil
½ cup toasted pine nuts
¾ cup shaved or shredded Parmesan cheese
Juice of ½ lemon
Salt to taste

1   Toss arugula with olive oil until coated.

2   Add pine nuts and Parmesan, and toss lightly.

3   Add lemon juice and season if desired. Toss gently and serve.

Prep time: *5 minutes,* **Serves** *4*

Nutrition Snapshot
Per serving: 328 calories, 31 g fat, 6 g saturated fat, 11 g protein, 5 g carbs, 1 g fiber, 1 g sugar, 303 mg sodium

Harvest Grains Vegetable Soup

Harvest Grains is a Trader Joe's bagged combination of Israeli couscous (also known as pearl couscous), red quinoa, baby garbanzo beans, and orzo. It's a wonderful, quick cooking pilaf to use in place of rice. It also makes a satisfying soup that you can customize with your own blend of vegetables. The best part is that it's ready in minutes. If you have fresh herbs on hand, such as parsley, basil, or thyme, add a tablespoon or two right before you serve the soup.

4 cups (one 32-oz carton) vegetable broth
1 cup thinly sliced celery
1 cup thinly sliced carrots
½ cup Harvest Grains
Salt and pepper to taste

1 Add broth to a medium saucepan and bring to a boil.

2 Add vegetables and grains. Bring to a boil and simmer for 15 minutes, skimming if needed. Add extra water or broth if soup becomes too thick.

3 Taste and adjust seasonings.

Prep time: *5 minutes*
Hands-off cooking time: *15 minutes*
Serves *4*

Nutrition Snapshot
Per serving: 122 calories, 1 g fat, 0 g saturated fat, 4 g protein, 25 g carbs, 3 g fiber, 6 g sugar, 182 mg sodium

Homemade Blue Cheese Dressing

We skipped the mayonnaise and sour cream used in traditional blue cheese dressings and created one using Greek yogurt and buttermilk. The star component of this dressing is tangy blue cheese, complemented with lemon and garlic. Enjoy this dressing over sweet and light lettuces, such as iceberg, Romaine, or butter lettuce. The dressing will keep for several days in the refrigerator in a covered container or jar.

4 oz (½ container) Crumbled Salem Blue cheese

½ cup cultured low-fat (1%) buttermilk

½ cup non-fat Greek yogurt

1 Tbsp lemon juice

1 clove garlic, crushed, or 1 cube frozen Crushed Garlic, thawed

Black pepper

Dried cranberries for garnish (optional)

1 Combine buttermilk, yogurt, lemon, and garlic. Gently stir in blue cheese and season to taste with pepper.

2 Serve dressing over butter lettuce or wedges of iceberg lettuce and garnish with cranberries.

Variation: *If using plain yogurt instead of thick Greek yogurt, use 1 cup plain yogurt and omit buttermilk or the dressing will be too runny.*

Prep time: *5 minutes*

Makes *10 (2-Tbsp) servings*

Nutrition Snapshot

Per serving (not including garnish): 52 calories, 3 g fat, 2 g saturated fat, 4 g protein, 2 g carbs, 0 g fiber, 1 g sugar, 173 mg sodium

Gluten Free

Winter Caprese (Beet and Mozzarella Salad)

During winter, when tomatoes aren't their best, try this twist on traditional Caprese Salad, the famous Italian dish made of tomato slices, mozzarella slices, and fresh basil. Ready-cooked beets and pre-sliced mozzarella take all the work out of this dish.

1 (8-oz) pkg refrigerated Steamed and Peeled Baby Beets, sliced

8 oz Mozzarella Medallions (about ⅔ of the 12-oz pkg), or slice your own fresh mozzarella

1 Tbsp olive oil

2 tsp lemon juice or white wine vinegar

1 Tbsp fresh basil, julienned or chopped

Salt and black pepper

1   Arrange beets and mozzarella slices in alternating pattern on serving dish. Be careful with the beets – the juice will stain.

2   Whisk together olive oil and lemon juice. Pour evenly over beets and mozzarella.

3   Sprinkle basil liberally over entire dish. Sprinkle on salt and pepper to taste.

Prep time: *10 minutes*
Serves *8*

Nutrition Snapshot

Per serving: 109 calories, 8 g fat, 4 g saturated fat, 6 g protein, 3 g carbs, 1 g fiber, 2 g sugar, 122 mg sodium

G
Gluten Free

Stuffed Red Peppers 78

Pasta alla Checca 81

Black Bean Burger 82

Hurry for Curry 85

Portabella Bunless Burger 86

Grilled Veggie Sandwich with Lemon Garlic Sauce 89

Thai Pizza 90

Corny-Copia Bean and Veggie Casserole 92

Portabella "Philly Cheesesteak" 94

Boursin Roasted Red Pepper Penne 97

Vegetable Tikka Masala 98

Anytime Mediterranean Pasta 101

Roasted Red Pepper and Mozzarella Sandwich 102

Easy Tofu Stir Fry 104

Stir-Fried Pasta with Sun Dried Tomatoes 106

Creamy Lemony Linguine 109

Soy Chorizo Chili 110

Southwest Burrito 113

Pesto Pita Pizza 114

Spicy Szechuan Tofu 117

Simply Quiche 118

Shiitake Mushroom Risotto 121

Eggplant Parmesan 122

Tamale Bake 125

Sushi Bowl 126

No-Prep Veggie Lasagna 128

Spinach Pesto Pasta Salad 131

Mushroom Moussaka 132

Black Bean and Ricotta-Stuffed Portabellas 135

South of the Border Pizza 136

Gyoza Salad 138

Gnutmeg Gnocchi with Spinach 141

Five-Minute Shiitake Fried Rice 142

Hummus and Lentil Wrap 145

White Lightning Chili 147

Addictive Tacos 148

Grilled Lentil Wraps 150

Spinach Ricotta Calzone 153

My Big Fat Greek Quiche 155

Mozzarella Basil Wrap 156

Arugula Pesto Pasta 159

Peanutty Sesame Noodles 160

Main Meals

Stuffed Red Peppers

Stuffed bell peppers are a delicious gourmet side or vegetarian main dish, but the stuffing is typically complex and time-consuming. We kept the complex taste but ditched the long prep time. We have two versions – one with flavorful croutons & tomatoes and one with a pine nut & mushroom risotto – and they're both easy!

2 large red bell peppers, halved lengthwise with seeds and pith removed
1 ½ cups chopped tomatoes (~3 Roma tomatoes)
1 ½ cups (half a bag) Parmesan Crisps or Cheese & Garlic Croutons, coarsely crushed
¾ cup refrigerated Fresh Bruschetta Sauce
⅔ cup Shredded 3 Cheese Blend

1   Preheat oven to 350° F.

2   Place pepper halves on oiled baking dish. Mix together tomato, crushed crisps, bruschetta, and cheese. Stuff this mixture inside pepper halves, compacting lightly.

3   Bake uncovered for 30-35 minutes or until cheese is melted and top is golden.

Prep time: *10 minutes*
Hands-off cooking time: *30-35 minutes*
Makes *4 stuffed pepper halves*

Nutrition Snapshot
Per stuffed pepper half: 190 calories, 10 g fat, 3 g saturated fat, 8 g protein, 18 g carbs, 3 g fiber, 8 g sugar, 397 mg sodium

Mushroom Risotto Stuffing
1 bag frozen Mushroom Risotto or Asparagus Risotto, about 2 cups cooked
½ cup toasted pine nuts
⅔ cup shredded or sliced mozzarella cheese

1   Prepare risotto according to package instructions. Mix in pine nuts.

2   Stuff red peppers with this mixture and top with cheese.

3   Bake as before.

Nutrition Snapshot
Per serving: 295 calories, 21 g fat, 6 g saturated fat, 10 g protein, 19 g carbs, 2 g fiber, 6 g sugar, 236 mg sodium

Pasta alla Checca

This style of pasta is a favorite all over Italy in the summer, when tomatoes and basil are at their peak. You don't have to cook a thing except for the pasta. Lovers of fresh sauces on pasta, rejoice! The mozzarella cheese will soften slightly with the heat of the pasta, making for chewy cheese balls dotted throughout.

8 oz (half a package) linguine or spaghetti pasta
1 (8-oz) container refrigerated Fresh Bruschetta Sauce
¼ cup grated Parmesan cheese
1 (8-oz) container Ciliegine, Fresh Mozzarella balls
¼ cup chopped basil

1   Cook pasta in salted water according to package directions. Drain.

2   Add bruschetta and Parmesan cheese. Mix well to coat pasta evenly.

3   Stir in mozzarella balls gently, being careful not to break them. Top with basil and serve immediately.

Prep time: *5 minutes*
Hands-off cooking time: *10 minutes*
Serves *4*

Nutrition Snapshot
Per serving: 421 calories, 19 g fat, 7 g saturated fat, 22 g protein, 46 g carbs, 2 g fiber, 7 g sugar, 430 mg sodium

G
Gluten Free

Use gluten-free pasta

Black Bean Burger

Refried black beans are transformed into flavorful patties and topped with fresh tomato bruschetta for a satisfying and protein-rich burger. These homemade vegetarian patties are a breeze to make, moist on the inside and pan-fried crispy on the edges. Enjoy the patties with bruschetta as shown here, or serve with all the traditional burger fixings.

1 (16-oz) can Refried Black Beans
1 cup bread crumbs
1 egg
2 Tbsp vegetable or olive oil
4 slices Havarti or provolone cheese (optional)
½ cup refrigerated Fresh Bruschetta Sauce
4 hamburger buns

1   In a large bowl, combine refried beans, bread crumbs, and egg; mix well using hands. Form four patties and set on waxed paper or a plate.

2   Heat oil in skillet and, when hot, add patties. Cook 3-4 minutes each side until browned, adding more oil if necessary. Top patties with cheese if desired and let melt.

3   Serve patties immediately on buns, topping each patty with 2 Tbsp bruschetta.

Prep time: *5 minutes*
Cooking time: *6-8 minutes*
Makes *4 burgers*

Nutrition Snapshot

Per serving: 585 calories, 17g fat, 3g saturated fat, 21g protein, 89g carbs, 10g fiber, 12g sugar, 1198mg sodium
Per patty only: 305 calories, 10g fat, 2g saturated fat, 13g protein, 42g carbs, 8g fiber, 3g sugar, 655mg sodium

Hurry for Curry

Curry sauces are complex and delicious, and they are a great way to creatively use leftover ingredients. Although bottled Thai Yellow Curry already has coconut milk in it, adding more coconut milk softens and delicately sweetens the curry. Light Coconut Milk is also easy on the calories; unlike heavy cream, coconut milk has 50 calories per ⅓ cup. Not too bad for a little added creaminess. Feel free to substitute whatever vegetables you have on hand. Serve with rice, couscous, or tandoori naan.

1 (11-oz) bottle Thai Yellow Curry
¾ cup Light Coconut Milk (about half the can)
1 (16-oz) container firm tofu, cut into bite-size pieces
1 ½ cups green beans, cut into 2-inch pieces
1 red bell pepper, cut into bite-size pieces
½ onion, cut into bite-size pieces
½ cup baby carrots or sliced carrots
½ cup mushrooms, halved or quartered
1 Tbsp fresh basil leaves, chopped

1   Pour curry and coconut milk into medium-sized saucepan. Stir to combine.

2   Add tofu and vegetables. Bring to a boil, reduce heat to simmer, and cook 10-12 minutes, or until vegetables are crisp-tender.

3   Stir in basil and remove from heat.

Prep time: *10 minutes,*
Hands-off cooking time: *10-12 minutes*
Serves *6*

Nutrition Snapshot
Per serving: 293 calories, 18 g fat, 6 g saturated fat, 13 g protein, 24 g carbs, 5 g fiber, 10 g sugar, 1067 mg sodium

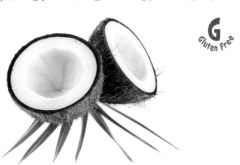

G
Gluten Free

Portabella Bunless Burger

Portabella mushrooms are a favorite because they're earthy, flavorful, hearty and meaty, making them popular in vegetarian dishes. Here, instead of using a bun, we top a mouth-watering mushroom cap with a Masala Veggie Burger, avocado slices, and micro greens—wonderful for a quick lunch or dinner. Romaine leaves will keep the veggie burger from soaking up the mushroom juices and getting soggy.

1 large Portabella mushroom cap, stem removed
1 frozen Veggie Masala Burger
1 Tbsp olive oil, divided
Pinch each salt and black pepper
Romaine leaves
¼ ripe avocado, sliced
Handful Organic Micro Greens

1   Coat Portabella cap with ½ Tbsp oil and sprinkle with salt and pepper. Heat remaining oil in large skillet over medium heat. Place Portabella cap and Veggie Masala burger side by side in skillet; cook both for 3-4 minutes on each side until Portabella cap is soft and burger is heated through.

2   Transfer Portabella cap to plate and top with Romaine leaves, veggie burger, avocado, and micro greens.

Prep and cooking time: *10 minutes*
Serves *1*

Nutrition Snapshot
Per serving: 222 calories, 15g fat, 2g saturated fat, 5g protein, 20g carbs, 5g fiber, 3g sugar, 369mg sodium

Gluten Free

Helpful Tip: *To make your own Misto Alla Griglia, slice zucchini and eggplant into ¼-inch-thick pieces, coat with olive oil, and sprinkle with salt and pepper. Grill or pan-sauté until tender.*

Grilled Veggie Sandwich with Lemon Garlic Sauce

In this sandwich, rich eggplant and zucchini slices contrast with fresh, peppery arugula and tangy feta. Trader Joe's Misto Alla Griglia (Grilled Eggplant & Zucchini) takes all the work out of preparing the grilled veggies. The measurements are approximate – use more veggies per sandwich if desired. For a picnic or party batch, see note below for making multiple sandwiches. Don't skip the lemon garlic sauce - it adds incredible flavor.

¼ (16-oz) bag frozen Misto Alla Griglia (Marinated Grilled Eggplant & Zucchini)
1 Petits Pains Rustiques (large Country Style French Rolls)
½ cup fresh arugula, loosely packed
1 Tbsp Crumbled Feta with Mediterranean Herbs

Lemon Garlic Sauce
1 Tbsp mayonnaise
1 tsp lemon juice
1 cube frozen Crushed Garlic or 1 small clove garlic, crushed

1 Thaw Misto alla Griglia overnight in fridge or microwave per package instructions. Use cold or heat in microwave until warm.

2 Cut roll in half.

3 In a small bowl, stir together ingredients for Lemon Garlic Sauce until smooth.

4 Build sandwich by drizzling sauce onto bottom of roll. Add arugula, eggplant and zucchini slices, and finish with a topping of feta. Cut in half and serve.

Prep time: *10 minutes*
Serves *2*

Nutrition Snapshot
Per serving (half sandwich): 261 calories, 10 g fat, 2 g saturated fat,
7 g protein, 35 g carbs, 3 g fiber, 3 g sugar, 686 mg sodium

G
Gluten Free

Use gluten-free bread or gluten-free bagel

Note: *1 (16-oz) bag of Misto Alla Griglia and 1 (8-oz) bag of Petits Pains Rustiques is enough to make 4 large sandwiches (8 servings).*

Thai Pizza

Thai pizza combines the flavors and textures of Pad Thai noodles in a pizza. Delicious peanut sauce, teriyaki-flavored baked tofu, and shredded mozzarella are baked hot on a crust. The pizza is then topped with crunchy fresh carrots, sweet snap peas, green onion, and cilantro. The silky smooth peanut sauce is easy to make using Trader Joe's Soyaki teriyaki sauce, and other shortcuts include ready-to-use pizza dough and pre-shredded carrots.

1 (1-lb) bag refrigerated Ready to Bake Pizza Dough

1 (3.5-oz) piece Organic Baked Tofu, Teriyaki Flavor (optional)

1 cup shredded mozzarella cheese

1 cup Shredded Carrots

1 cup sliced sugar snap peas

¼ cup chopped green onion

2 Tbsp chopped fresh cilantro (optional)

Sweet Chili Sauce (optional)

Peanut Sauce

2 Tbsp Soyaki or other teriyaki sauce

¼ cup smooth unsalted peanut butter

1 Tbsp toasted sesame oil

1 tsp honey

3 Tbsp water

1 Preheat oven to 450° F. Make sure oven is preheated for at least 20 minutes, especially if using a pizza stone.

2 Roll out dough into a 12–inch circle. Bake on lightly oiled baking sheet or pizza stone for 5 minutes. Remove parbaked crust from oven and set aside while you prepare the peanut sauce.

3 Whisk together all Peanut Sauce ingredients until smooth. Spread sauce evenly over pizza crust. Crumble tofu with fingers onto crust. Sprinkle with mozzarella. Return to oven and bake for 8 minutes longer until cheese is melted and bubbly.

4 Remove pizza from oven and top with shredded carrots, snap peas, green onion, and cilantro. Drizzle with Sweet Chili Sauce if desired. Slice and serve immediately.

Prep time: *10 minutes*
Hands-off cooking time: *13 minutes*
Serves *4*

Nutrition Snapshot

Per ¼ pizza: 528 calories, 20 g fat, 6 g saturated fat, 23 g protein, 66 g carbs, 5 g fiber, 4 g sugar, 609 mg sodium

Corny-Copia Bean and Veggie Casserole

This dish is a complex and substantial vegetarian entrée, layered with beans, grilled vegetables, and a cornbread topping. It was adapted from a recipe in the Moosewood Cookbook, which required an hour and a half of preparation. We've come up with a version we like just as well that can be made in a fraction of the time.

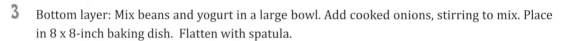

1 medium yellow onion, chopped, or 1 ½ cups bagged Freshly Diced Onions
1 clove garlic, crushed, or 1 cube frozen Crushed Garlic
2 Tbsp extra virgin olive oil
1 tsp ground cumin
1 (15-oz) can pinto beans, drained completely
½ cup plain yogurt
1 (12-oz) jar Fire Roasted Red & Yellow Peppers, drained and chopped
1 (10-oz) jar Green Olive Tapenade or other olive tapenade/bruschetta
1 (15-oz) box Cornbread Mix, prepared to instructions and set aside

1   Preheat oven to 375° F.

2   Sauté onions, garlic and cumin in olive oil until onions are soft and translucent. Set pan aside to cool.

3   Bottom layer: Mix beans and yogurt in a large bowl. Add cooked onions, stirring to mix. Place in 8 x 8-inch baking dish. Flatten with spatula.

4   Middle layer: Mix together peppers and tapenade; spread over bean mixture.

5   Top casserole with a thin layer of cornbread batter (about ⅔ of the mix —use the rest to make muffins for breakfast the next day). Spoon cornbread batter evenly and thinly over the top, taking care not to disturb the layers.

6   Bake uncovered for 35-40 minutes or until cornbread is fully cooked and golden brown.

Variation: *For the middle layer, substitute 2 cups of Oven Roasted Vegetables (see p. 172)*

Prep time: *15 minutes*
Hands-off cooking time: *35-40 minutes*
Serves *9*

Nutrition Snapshot
Per serving: 437 calories, 21 g fat, 1 g saturated fat, 7 g protein, 54 g carbs, 4 g fiber, 20 g sugar, 829 mg sodium

Portabella "Philly Cheesesteak"

The iconic cheesesteak hails from Philadelphia where it became a regional classic. Our scrumptious version is made with meaty Portabella slices. The filling comes together quickly with ready-to-use frozen fire-roasted peppers and onions and a touch of garlic. Topped with melted cheese and served on a toasted bun, this classic is sure to become a favorite in your home.

1 large Portabella mushroom cap, stem removed and sliced thinly

2 cups frozen Fire Roasted Peppers and Onions

1 Tbsp olive oil

1 Tbsp soy sauce

1 clove garlic, crushed, or 1 cube frozen Crushed Garlic

2 slices Provolone cheese

2 Panini Rolls or other buns, toasted

1 Heat oil in a skillet over medium-high heat. Add sliced mushroom and frozen peppers and onions. Drizzle with soy sauce and add garlic. Cook and stir until mushroom slices are soft and veggies are heated through (about 2 minutes).

2 Place cheese on top of mushroom mixture in pan and continue to heat until cheese is melted. Divide filling between buns and serve hot.

Prep and cooking time: *10 minutes*
Makes *2 sandwiches*

Nutrition Snapshot
Per sandwich: 350 calories, 15g fat, 6g saturated fat, 13g protein, 41g carbs, 4g fiber, 7g sugar, 689mg sodium

Boursin Roasted Red Pepper Penne

Veronica O'Neill of VoKnits.com sent us this delicious gourmet recipe. When asked how she came up with it, she said it was just one of those whatever-you-have-in-the-fridge kind of recipes that she made up on the fly. Her son was very young at the time, and he liked that it was sweet and could be eaten using his fingers. Now that he's older (and using a fork), they often have it served warm on a bed of wild arugula.

1 (16-oz) pkg penne pasta
1 (12-oz) jar Fire Roasted Red Peppers, drained and sliced
1 (5.2-oz) pkg Boursin Garlic & Fine Herbs Gournay Cheese, softened
4 oz (½ block) Neufchâtel or cream cheese, softened
Dash black pepper

1 Cook penne according to package directions in salted water.

2 While pasta is cooking, assemble cream sauce. Over very low heat, melt cheeses together and blend. Be sure to use very low heat to avoid scorching cheeses. Add a ladle of boiling water (from pasta pot) to thin out cream sauce.

3 Drain pasta and add cream sauce and roasted peppers. Stir to coat evenly.

4 Serve with a dash of cracked black pepper.

Prep time: *10 minutes*
Cook time: *10 minutes*
Serves *6*

Nutrition Snapshot
Per serving: 421 calories, 15 g fat, 9 g saturated fat, 9 g protein, 63 g carbs, 4 g fiber, 1 g sugar, 272 mg sodium

Use gluten-free pasta

Vegetable Tikka Masala

Tikka Masala is one of our favorite Indian dishes. Masala is a slightly spicy tomato-based sauce that is commonly believed to be a product of Indian-British fusion cooking, although the origins are somewhat unclear. When you combine it with the cooling taste of yogurt, you get a Tikka Masala sauce that is nicely balanced, complex and very creamy but not heavy. It's great served over plain steamed basmati rice or quinoa, along with some Tandoori Naan (available fresh or frozen in several flavors).

1 (15-oz) jar Masala Simmer Sauce

1 (12-oz) bag Cauliflower Florets or 3 cups cauliflower, cut into bite-size pieces

1 medium zucchini, unpeeled, diced into ½ inch chunks (about 1 cup)

½ cup frozen peas

¾ cup canned garbanzo beans

½ cup carrots, thinly sliced (optional)

½ cup plain yogurt, such as Plain Cream Line Yogurt

1. Pour masala sauce in a wide large saucepan over medium heat.

2. Add cauliflower, zucchini, peas, garbanzo beans, and carrots. Stir until all ingredients are coated.

3. Once simmering, cover pan and turn heat to medium-low. Simmer for an additional 12-15 minutes or until cauliflower and carrots are just tender.

4. Ladle out ½ cup or more of the curry and mix into the yogurt (this will temper the yogurt, so that it doesn't curdle in the hot curry). Stir yogurt mixture into the pan, bring to a simmer again, and then remove from heat.

Prep time: *5 minutes*
Hands off cooking time: *15-20 minutes*
Serves *4*

Nutrition Snapshot

Per serving: 175 calories, 5 g fat, 1 g saturated fat, 9 g protein, 27 g carbs, 7 g fiber, 14 g sugar, 592 mg sodium

Anytime Mediterranean Pasta

This pasta dish can be your fallback option even if your fridge is nearly bare. Just keep a bag of pasta, a bag of pine nuts, and a few jarred sauces on hand in your pantry. Parmesan cheese will keep for a long time in your fridge.

3 cups (half a bag) fusilli pasta
½ cup pitted Kalamata olives
2 Tbsp Julienne Sliced Sun Dried Tomatoes
⅓ cup toasted pine nuts
2 Tbsp Pesto alla Genovese Basil Pesto
¼ cup grated or shredded Parmesan cheese

1   Cook pasta according to package instructions and drain.
2   Stir in remaining ingredients, topping with Parmesan as desired.

Prep and cooking time: *15 minutes*
Serves *4*

Nutrition Snapshot
Per serving: 368 calories, 17 g fat, 2 g saturated fat, 7 g protein, 50 g carbs, 3 g fiber, 2 g sugar, 226 mg sodium

G
Gluten Free

Use gluten-free pasta

Roasted Red Pepper and Mozzarella Sandwich

You'd expect to see this gourmet sandwich served at a fancy café, and it takes just minutes to make. Roasted peppers taste great right out of the jar and are even better when combined with fresh mozzarella medallions. Serve this sandwich with colorful tomatoes, veggie chips, or fresh fruit for a gourmet lunch in a snap.

1 serving crusty bread, or 1 Organic Miniature Baguette

1-2 pieces Fire Roasted Red or Yellow Bell Peppers

3 pieces Fresh Mozzarella Medallions, or sliced fresh mozzarella cheese

1 tsp balsamic vinegar

4 fresh basil leaves

Salt and black pepper

1 Slice baguette open; toast if desired.

2 Drizzle or brush balsamic vinegar on one side of bread. Layer on roasted red peppers, mozzarella, and basil.

3 Sprinkle with salt and pepper to taste. Close sandwich and serve.

Prep time: *5 minutes*
Serves *1*

Nutrition Snapshot

Per serving: 248 calories, 9 g fat, 5 g saturated fat, 12 g protein, 29 g carbs, 1 g fiber, 3 g sugar, 555 mg sodium

*Use gluten-free bread
or gluten-free bagel*

Easy Tofu Stir Fry

It's good to have a wide variety of easy recipes using fresh vegetables that can be a quick 10-minutes-to-the-table dinner, like this easy tofu-based stir fry. Tofu is lightly flavored with sesame oil and gets a tiny bit of heat from chili oil. Vegetables are crisp and vibrant in the tasty soy-teriyaki sauce. Serve over brown or white rice.

½ brick tofu (regular), cut into ½-inch cubes and drained

1 Tbsp olive oil

1 tsp toasted sesame oil

10 drops chili oil

4 cups Stir Fry Vegetables (Napa cabbage variety) or substitute an equivalent amount of broccoli florets, white cabbage, and/or bok choy

⅓ cup Soyaki or Veri Veri Teriyaki

1   Heat a wok or wide saucepan on high and add all oils. Add tofu and stir-fry for 2 minutes.

2   Reduce heat to medium-high, add vegetables and Soyaki, and continue to stir-fry for an additional 3 minutes or until broccoli is bright green.

Prep and cooking time: *15 minutes*
Serves *4*

Nutrition Snapshot

Per serving: 193 calories, 12 g fat, 1 g saturated fat, 8 g protein, 13 g carbs, 3 g fiber, 7 g sugar, 716 mg sodium

Stir-Fried Pasta with Sun Dried Tomatoes

When Deana was in graduate school, her housemate Tom would make a dish very similar to this pasta. Tom was a good cook and also the only male grad student she'd ever met who had a subscription to *Bon Appétit* magazine. The ingredients in this dish are simple, but they come together with a fabulous toasty flavor from the light stir-frying of the pasta.

1 (16-oz) bag fusilli pasta
1 (8.5-oz) jar Julienne Sliced Sun Dried Tomatoes
½ cup packed finely chopped Italian parsley
⅔ cup toasted pine nuts
¾ cup shredded Parmesan cheese

1 In a large pot, boil pasta in salted water according to instructions on bag. Drain completely.

2 Drain jar of sun dried tomatoes and reserve drained oil (nearly ½ cup!). In the same large pot as before, heat 4 Tbsp of this oil over high heat. Add pasta and stir with a spatula or spoon. Stir-fry pasta for a couple minutes, stirring to keep pasta moving around. Don't worry if pasta starch sticks to the bottom and browns/toasts.

3 Remove pasta from heat and add sun dried tomatoes, parsley, pine nuts, and Parmesan. Toss together and serve.

Prep time and cooking time: *15-20 minutes*
Serves *8*

Nutrition Snapshot

Per serving: 436 calories, 20 g fat, 4 g saturated fat, 12 g protein, 57 g carbs, 4 g fiber, 8 g sugar, 221 mg sodium

G Gluten Free

Use gluten-free pasta

Note: *Don't fret about the pot being hard to clean. Any pasta starch stuck to the bottom of the pan will wash right out after 5-10 minutes of soaking. Really! Use the remaining reserved oil to sauté veggies or add to another dish.*

Creamy Lemony Linguine

Linguine flavored with mushrooms and a zingy lemon pepper cream sauce is a tasty entrée. This recipe doesn't rely on seasonal ingredients, and it's a snap to make. The Trader Joe's Lemon Pepper seasoning gives it a tasty kick without over-powering the subtle flavor of mushrooms. (We can't guarantee good results using other brands of lemon pepper seasoning, which may have peculiar aftertastes, according to one of our testers.) Serve with a green salad.

1 (16-oz) box or bag linguine pasta
1 cup heavy cream or whipping cream
½ cup shaved or shredded Parmesan cheese
Juice of 1 lemon (2 Tbsp)
2 tsp Lemon Pepper (in a grinder container)
2 Tbsp butter, unsalted
1 (10-oz) container sliced white mushrooms

1   Prepare linguine according to package instructions.

2   While linguine cooks, prepare the sauce. In a small saucepan over medium heat, pour in heavy cream and add Parmesan, stirring until Parmesan is melted into the cream. Stir in lemon juice and lemon pepper. Turn heat to lowest setting while you prepare the mushrooms.

3   In a hot skillet, melt butter and add mushrooms. Cook for 1 minute, stirring constantly, and take off heat before mushrooms give off any water. You want to keep mushrooms plump and firm, not stewed and shrunken.

4   Drain pasta when done and place in a large bowl. Pour sauce over pasta, add mushrooms, and toss together until sauce is evenly distributed.

5   Top with more Parmesan and serve.

Prep and cooking time: *15-20 minutes*
Serves *8*

Nutrition Snapshot
Per serving: 370 calories, 16 g fat, 10 g saturated fat, 12 g protein, 46 g carbs, 3 g fiber, 4 g sugar, 153 mg sodium

Use gluten-free pasta

Soy Chorizo Chili

Arriba! This spicy chorizo version of a classic needs no extra chili powder to kick up the flavor. This recipe makes a large batch that is perfect for parties and large gatherings, but you can easily cut in half.

1 pkg Soy Chorizo
1 tsp olive oil
1 medium onion, chopped
1 (28-oz) can diced tomatoes
1 cup vegetable broth or water
2 (15-oz) cans beans of your choice (pinto, black, kidney), drained
1 (15-oz) can corn or 1 cup frozen corn kernels
1 bell pepper, diced
1 tsp sugar (optional)

1 Heat olive oil in a pot over medium-high heat. Add onions and sauté until softened, about 5 minutes.

2 Add all remaining ingredients and heat to boiling. Reduce heat, cover, and simmer on low for 15-20 minutes.

3 Serve with your choice of toppings, such as cilantro, green onions, sour cream, shredded cheese, avocados, tortilla chips.

Prep and cooking time: *15 minutes*
Serves *4*

Nutrition Snapshot
Per serving: 368 calories, 17 g fat, 2 g saturated fat, 7 g protein, 50 g carbs, 3 g fiber, 2 g sugar, 226 mg sodium

Use gluten-free broth

Southwest Burrito

A flour tortilla wrapped around black beans, veggies, cheese, and salsa makes a perfect meal anytime. You'll be surprised at the burst of flavor in this healthy, low-fat burrito.

1 large flour tortilla

3 heaping Tbsp canned black beans, drained

A few pieces of Oven Roasted Vegetables (page 172), Fire Roasted Red Peppers or Fire Roasted Yellow & Red Peppers

3 Tbsp Fancy Shredded Mexican Blend cheese

2 Tbsp Chunky Salsa

A few sprigs fresh cilantros

Slices of fresh avocado (optional)

Dollop of sour cream or yogurt (optional)

1   Place all ingredients down the center of the tortilla.

2   Roll tightly.

Prep time: *5 minutes*
Serves *1*

Nutrition Snapshot
Per serving: 211 calories, 4 g fat, 0 g saturated fat, 8 g protein, 36 g carbs, 3 g fiber, 2 g sugar, 633 mg sodium

Pesto Pita Pizza

These easy individual-size pizzas are a breeze to assemble using pita pockets that bake up delicious and crispy on the edges. The best part is that each pizza can be customized using your own choice of toppings. Adding fresh tomato and basil after baking creates a garden-fresh contrast to the hot, crisp pizza.

2 standard-size (7-inch diameter) pita pockets
4 Tbsp refrigerated Genova Pesto or jarred Pesto alla Genovese
½ cup shredded mozzarella cheese
1 ripe tomato, diced (about ½ cup)
2 Tbsp chopped fresh basil

1 Preheat oven to 400° F.

2 Place pitas on baking sheet, lightly sprayed with cooking oil.

3 Spread 2 Tbsp pesto on each pita. Top each with ¼ cup of cheese.

4 Bake for 8 minutes, until cheese is bubbly.

5 Remove from oven and top with tomato and basil.

Variation: *Use marinara (or tomato sauce), black olives, and mozzarella.*

Prep time: *5 minutes*
Hands-off cooking time: *8 minutes*
Serves *2*

Nutrition Snapshot

Per serving: 321 calories, 17 g fat, 3 g saturated fat,
10 g protein, 31 g carbs, 2 g fiber, 2 g sugar, 388 mg sodium

Spicy Szechuan Tofu

This dish was inspired by Ma Po Tofu, a spicy specialty from the Szechuan province of China. Although Ma Po Tofu is usually made with ground pork, we think this version is just as tasty with Trader Joe's Meatless Ground Beef. The sauce is sweet and mildly spiced, a favorite with kids.

1 (16-oz or 19-oz) pkg firm tofu, cut into ½-inch cubes
1 cup (half a 12-oz pkg) Beef-less Ground Beef
1 tsp vegetable oil
1 clove garlic, crushed, or 1 cube frozen Crushed Garlic
1 tsp crushed ginger
1 cup frozen peas
½ cup General Tsao Stir Fry Sauce
1 Tbsp soy sauce
1 tsp toasted sesame oil
2 green onions, chopped

1   Heat oil in a skillet or wok. Add Beef-less Ground Beef, garlic, ginger, and peas. Cook 3 minutes.

2   Add tofu, stir fry sauce, soy sauce, and sesame oil. Cook for 3 minutes or until heated through.

3   Add green onions and remove from heat. Serve over steamed white rice.

Prep and cooking time: *15 minutes*
Serves *4*

Nutrition Snapshot
Per serving: 253 calories, 8 g fat, 2 g saturated fat, 21 g protein, 27 g carbs, 4 g fiber, 18 g sugar, 723 mg sodium

Simply Quiche

Remember that '80s maxim "Real men don't eat quiche"? Well, we know that real men don't care about the macho rating of food, but they do care about protein. Quiche is healthy and sophisticated, and it will please any palate. It's a great main dish, from brunch to dinner. It's also easy to make, despite its fancy French culinary roots. Use this recipe as your foundation, and add other ingredients such as broccoli, olives, or herbs.

1 frozen pie crust, thawed and put into oven-safe pie dish
1 ½ cups crimini mushrooms, chopped or sliced
1 cup half and half
4 eggs
1 cup Quattro Formaggio shredded cheese
½ cup chopped canned or frozen artichoke hearts (not marinated!)
1 cup frozen spinach, thawed and water squeezed out (it will measure about ¼ cup packed)
⅛ tsp ground nutmeg
¼ tsp salt

1 Preheat oven to 375° F.

2 Sauté mushrooms in olive oil just until they start to brown, about 1 minute.

3 Whisk together eggs and half and half. Stir in mushrooms, cheese, artichoke hearts, spinach, nutmeg, and salt.

4 Pour mixture into pie crust and bake for 40 minutes, or until knife inserted into center comes out clean.

5 Allow to cool for a few minutes, then slice and serve.

Prep time: *10 minutes*
Hands-off cooking time: *40 minutes*
Serves 6

Nutrition Snapshot
Per serving: 286 calories, 20 g fat, 8 g saturated fat, 13 g protein, 15 g carbs, 1 g fiber, 1 g sugar, 529 mg sodium

Shiitake Mushroom Risotto

Risotto is a creamy rice dish made with Arborio rice. This delicious risotto is flavored with shiitake mushrooms, onion, garlic, wine, and garlic. The simple combination is fantastic without requiring heavy cream or lots of cheese for taste. Make sure that it is fluid and creamy when finished, not dry and stiff. When placed on a plate that is shaken side to side, risotto should spread and move.

2 cups Arborio rice

2 Tbsp extra virgin olive oil, divided

1 small onion, diced

1 (3.5-oz) pkg shiitake mushrooms, chopped (8 mushrooms or 1 ½ cups chopped)

1 clove garlic, crushed or 1 cube frozen Crushed Garlic

½ cup dry white wine

4 cups vegetable broth + 1 cup water

1 sprig fresh rosemary

Parmesan cheese (optional)

1 In a saucepan, add broth and water and bring to a simmer.

2 Heat 1 Tbsp oil in a pan or deep skillet over high heat. Add onion and saute until onion begins to soften (~3 minutes), lowering heat to medium.

3 Add mushrooms and garlic, stirring and cooking for 1-2 minutes until mushrooms are soft.

4 Add remaining 1 Tbsp oil and add rice, stirring well. Continuing stirring and cooking for 3-4 minutes, allowing rice to toast.

5 Add wine and stir until absorbed.

6 Ladle in 1 cup of broth and add rosemary, stirring. Lower the heat to a gentle simmer. Continue to add broth in 1-2 ladle increments, regularly stirring and allowing liquid to be mostly absorbed before adding more. All the liquid will be absorbed over the course of 20 minutes cooking time.

7 When cooked, the rice should be al dente and the risotto should be fluid and smooth. Add more broth or water if necessary. Garnish with Parmesan and serve immediately.

Prep time: *10 minutes*
Cooking time: *30 minutes*
Serves *4*

Nutrition Snapshot
Per serving: 283 calories, 7 g fat, 1 g saturated fat, 4 g protein, 43 g carbs, 3 g fiber, 5 g sugar, 141 mg sodium

Use gluten-free broth

Eggplant Parmesan

Eggplant Parmesan, also known as *melanzane alla parmigiana* or *eggplant parmigiana,* is a well-loved classic Italian dish originating in Naples. The time-consuming part of a traditional eggplant Parmesan recipe is the preparation of the eggplant cutlets, which need to be salted, rested, rinsed, breaded, and fried. With Trader Joe's frozen eggplant cutlets, suddenly the recipe is a snap. Use your favorite marinara, try different cheeses such as fresh mozzarella or ricotta, add a bag of thawed frozen spinach, or add fresh herbs to your liking. Serve with a green salad and crusty bread.

1 (1-lb) box frozen Eggplant Cutlets
1 (25-oz) jar marinara sauce
1 ½ cups shredded mozzarella cheese
½ cup shredded Parmesan cheese
Chopped fresh basil or parsley (optional)

1 Preheat oven to 375° F.

2 In the bottom of an 8 x 12 or 9 x 13-inch baking dish, spread one cup of marinara. Place frozen eggplant cutlets in the dish in one layer, overlapping as necessary.

3 Pour remaining marinara over eggplant cutlets, then sprinkle with the two cheeses.

4 Bake uncovered for 35 minutes. Remove from oven and let rest 5-10 minutes. Top with fresh herbs before serving.

Prep time: *5 minutes*
Hands-off cooking time: *35 minutes*
Serves *8*

Nutrition Snapshot
Per serving: 241 calories, 12 g fat, 4 g saturated fat, 12 g protein, 22 g carbs, 2 g fiber, 11 g sugar, 528 mg sodium

Sushi Bowl

When you want sushi and you want it now, try this easy deconstructed sushi in a bowl. No special rolling mat (or expertise) required. This is a great dish for a buffet spread because guests can customize their own toppings. In our home, it's a fun way to clean up leftover veggies that have accumulated during the week. For sinus-clearing spiciness, try it with Trader Joe's wasabi-flavored roasted seaweed.

2 (10-oz) pouches fully-cooked frozen Brown Rice, or 4 cups cooked rice

1 (7-oz) pkg baked tofu, teriyaki or any flavor, sliced into thin strips

1 cup cooked and shelled edamame

1 (0.4-oz) pkg Roasted Seaweed Snack, cut in strips or crushed into pieces

1 avocado, peeled and diced

2 tsp sesame seeds (optional)

Sauce
3 Tbsp rice wine vinegar

1 Tbsp Soyaki or teriyaki sauce

1   Reheat rice according to package instructions and divide into individual bowls. Place tofu, edamame, seaweed, and avocado in piles on top of rice. Sprinkle with sesame seeds.

2   Whisk vinegar and Soyaki in a small bowl. Drizzle over sushi bowl.

Prep time: *10 minutes*
Serves *4*

Nutrition Snapshot
Per serving: 476 calories, 14 g fat, 3 g saturated fat, 19 g protein, 72 g carbs, 10 g fiber, 7 g sugar, 796 mg sodium

Tamale Bake

Inspired by tamales, this quick and easy casserole features polenta, the Italian version of Southern grits. Polenta is firm and crumbly when cold, but is transformed into soft layers of chewy goodness when heated. Using pre-cooked polenta sold in formed tubes makes this delicious casserole a snap. Experiment with other vegetables such as butternut squash, bell peppers, or eggplant, and other cheeses such as goat cheese, to create a myriad of tasty variations.

2 (18-oz) tubes pre-cooked polenta, each tube sliced into 9 rounds

2 Tbsp olive oil

1 large onion, chopped, or 2 cups refrigerated Diced Onions

3 zucchini squash, sliced

1 (12-oz) pkg Soy Chorizo, removed from casing, or substitute 1 pkg Beef-Less Ground Beef cooked in 1 tsp Taco Seasoning or ⅓ cup Enchilada Sauce or Chunky Salsa

2 (15-oz) cans black beans, drained

½ cup Enchilada Sauce

1 cup Fancy Shredded Mexican Blend cheese

¼ cup fresh cilantro, chopped

Sour cream as garnish (optional)

1   Preheat oven to 350° F.

2   Heat olive oil in a skillet. Sauté onion and zucchini until soft, about 5 minutes. Add chorizo and stir. Remove from heat.

3   Lightly oil a square baking dish. Place half the polenta on the bottom, overlapping as necessary. Sprinkle on half each of the chorizo mixture, black beans, enchilada sauce, and shredded cheese. Repeat with the 2nd layer.

4   Cover and bake for 30 minutes until cheese is melted and casserole is piping hot. Sprinkle cilantro evenly on top. Serve with sour cream.

Prep time: *20 minutes*
Hands-off cooking time: *30 minutes*
Serves *8*

Nutrition Snapshot

Per serving: 361 calories, 16 g fat, 4 g saturated fat, 17 g protein, 42 g carbs, 9 g fiber, 6 g sugar, 1080 mg sodium

Gluten Free

Use your favorite salsa instead of Enchilada Sauce

No-Prep Veggie Lasagna

This no-prep eggplant and spinach lasagna takes advantage of a bunch of great shortcuts, eliminating the sink full of dirty pots and pans that usually follow a batch of lasagna. It only requires a few minutes of prep time before it goes into the oven. For maximum efficiency, place bags of frozen Misto alla Griglia (Grilled Eggplant & Zucchini) and frozen spinach in the fridge the night before, so they'll be thawed and ready to use.

½ (16-oz) box No Boil Lasagna Noodles
2 (26-oz) jars Tomato Basil Marinara
1 (15-oz) container ricotta
1 (16-oz) bag frozen chopped spinach, thawed
1 (16-oz) bag frozen Misto all Griglia (Grilled Eggplant & Zucchini), thawed
1 (14-oz) can artichoke hearts, drained and chopped (optional)
3 cups shredded mozzarella
¼ cup Parmesan or grated Pecorino Romano
Fresh basil or Italian parsley for garnish (optional)

1   Preheat oven to 350° F .

2   Cover bottom of 8x12-inch or 9x13-inch baking dish with ½ cup marinara. Put down one layer of noodles (three noodles for each layer works nicely).

3   Spread half the container of ricotta over noodles.

4   Squeeze spinach to remove excess water. Layer half the spinach on top of ricotta. Top with Misto alla Griglia slices and artichoke hearts. Pour on $1/3$ of the marinara. Sprinkle with 1 cup mozzarella.

5   Top with another layer of noodles, remaining ricotta, remaining spinach, remaining Misto slices and artichoke hearts. Pour on $1/3$ of the marinara. Sprinkle with 1 cup mozzarella.

6   Top with another layer of noodles, remaining marinara, and remaining mozzarella. Sprinkle with Parmesan.

7   Bake, covered with foil, for 30 minutes. Remove foil and bake for an additional 20 minutes, or until top is bubbling and melted. Let lasagna cool for a few minutes before serving so it will hold its shape. Garnish with herbs.

Prep time: *10 minutes*
Cooking time: *50 minutes*
Serves *8*

Nutrition Snapshot
Per serving: 279 calories, 7 g fat, 1 g saturated fat, 6 g protein, 40 g carbs, 2 g fiber, 2 g sugar, 555 mg sodium

Note: *Make sure to thaw completely any frozen ingredients before layering it in the lasagna. Don't be shy about using your hands when you make lasagna. You may find it easier to spread ricotta and spinach with your fingers, and press down with your hands to even out lasagna layers.*

Spinach Pesto Pasta Salad

The most popular flavors of Italy are combined in this colorful pasta salad. Pesto, cherry tomatoes, pine nuts, and mozzarella balls complement fresh baby spinach. This is a convenient make-ahead dish for a large crowd.

1 (16-oz) bag fusilli pasta
1 (7-oz) container refrigerated Genova Pesto
3 oz (½ bag) baby spinach
1 (16-oz) container heirloom cherry tomato mix
½ cup toasted pine nuts
1 (8-oz) container Ciliegine fresh mozzarella balls, drained

1   In a large pot, boil pasta in salted water according to instructions on bag. Drain completely.

2   In a large bowl, add pasta and pesto. Stir to distribute pesto throughout the pasta. Add spinach, tomatoes, pine nuts, and mozzarella balls. Stir gently to combine.

Prep and cooking time: *15 minutes*
Serves *8*

Nutrition Snapshot
Per serving: 456 calories, 24 g fat, 4 g saturated fat, 14 g protein, 51 g carbs, 5 g fiber, 0 g sugar, 104 mg sodium

Use gluten-free pasta

Mushroom Moussaka

This moussaka is a streamlined version of one in Mollie Katzen's *Moosewood Cookbook*. The only fuss here is the eggplant preparation, but it's well worth it. The classic version of moussaka is topped with creamy bechamel sauce, but we couldn't bring ourselves to top off all those healthy ingredients with fat and flour. Instead, we've captured its flavors by making a sauce out of yogurt, nutmeg, and Parmesan. It's a hearty meal that will satisfy even meat-lovers, and it's so delicious, you won't miss the fat.

3 large eggplants, unpeeled and sliced into thin ¼-inch rounds
2 trimmed leeks, chopped (about 3 cups)
1 (10-oz) bag sliced Crimini mushrooms
1 (24-oz) jar Rustico Southern Italian Sauce
1 tsp cinnamon
1 packed cup chopped parsley
½ cup shredded Parmesan cheese

Sauce
1 cup yogurt
¼ tsp nutmeg
½ cup shredded Parmesan cheese

1. Salt eggplant slices, making sure both sides are lightly covered, and place in a colander. Let sit for at least 15 minutes, preferably 30.

2. Preheat oven to 450° F. Add 1 Tbsp olive oil to a deep skillet over medium-high heat. Sauté leeks for 4 minutes. Add mushrooms and sauté for an additional 3-4 minutes. Add sauce and cinnamon. Bring to a simmer and then remove from heat. Stir in parsley and Parmesan.

3. Rinse eggplant slices and pat dry. Brush slices with olive oil and then spread on two baking sheets. Roast in oven for about 15 minutes until slices look softened.

4. Reduce oven to 375° F. Oil an 8x12 or 9x13-inch baking dish. Place two layers of eggplant slices in the bottom and add mushroom sauce on top. Cover with remaining eggplant slices (another two layers).

5. In a small bowl, mix yogurt, nutmeg, and Parmesan. Pour this over top of casserole and spread evenly.

6. Bake casserole, uncovered, for 40 minutes. Remove from oven and let rest 5 minutes before serving.

Prep time: *20 minutes, plus 15-30 minutes for salted eggplant to sit and sweat*
Hands-off cooking time: *15 + 40 minutes*
Serves *8*

Nutrition Snapshot
Per serving: 174 calories, 5 g fat, 3 g saturated fat, 12 g protein,
24 g carbs, 9 g fiber, 13 g sugar, 580 mg sodium

Black Bean and Ricotta-Stuffed Portabellas

Everyone who first sees this recipe thinks, "Black beans and ricotta – are you sure?" but follow up with, "Wow, it really works!" We wouldn't steer you wrong. The fillings have lots of complementary flavors and textures, and the Portabellas are a hearty and substantial base. This tasty recipe can really do triple duty as an appetizer, side dish, or light dinner.

2 large Portabella mushroom caps
½ cup ricotta cheese
½ cup canned black beans
2 Tbsp refrigerated Fresh Bruschetta Sauce
½ cup shredded mozzarella cheese

1 Preheat oven to 400° F.

2 Don't wash the Portabellas. Instead use a mushroom brush or a clean kitchen towel to wipe the caps.

3 Cut stems completely off the Portabella caps, and place caps upside down on an oiled baking sheet or pan. Combine ricotta and black beans. Spread this mixture inside the caps. Do not overfill since caps will shrink slightly as they cook. Add 1 Tbsp bruschetta sauce on top of the filling and top each cap with mozzarella.

4 Bake for 12-14 minutes. Do not overcook or the Portabellas will cook down and get very watery. Serve immediately.

Prep time: *5 minutes*
Hands-off cooking time: *12-14 minutes*
Serves *2*

Nutrition Snapshot
Per serving: 341 calories, 16 g fat, 11 g saturated fat, 27 g protein, 18 g carbs, 5 g fiber, 3 g sugar, 434 mg sodium

Tip: *Depending on the size of your Portabellas, you may have leftover filling. Don't toss it. The next morning, fill a tortilla with the mixture and some bruschetta and take it along for lunch. Use the leftover bruschetta and some goat cheese to top rice crackers.*

Gluten Free

South of the Border Pizza

A cool layer of guacamole on top of yummy hot beans, melted cheese, salsa, and a thin crust. This unique cold/hot pizza makes so much sense. Don't skip the cilantro—it really completes this pizza!

1 (1-lb) bag refrigerated Almost Whole Wheat Pizza Dough
1 (15-oz) can pinto beans, drained completely
½ cup Chunky Salsa
1 cup Shredded 3 Cheese Blend
1 cup (one tray) refrigerated Avocado's Number Guacamole
¼ cup chopped fresh cilantro

1   Preheat oven to 500° F or as high as your oven goes, preferably with a pizza stone inside.

2   Roll dough into a 12-inch circle on a lightly floured surface. Cover dough with salsa, beans, and cheese, in that order.

3   Transfer to pizza stone or baking sheet. Bake for 10 minutes or until cheese is bubbly.

4   Remove pizza from the oven and slice. Spread guacamole over each slice while hot, and sprinkle cilantro on top. Serve immediately.

Prep time: *10 minutes*
Hands-off cooking time: *10 minutes*
Serves *4*

Nutrition Snapshot
Per ¼-pizza: 562 calories, 19 g fat, 6 g saturated fat, 22 g protein, 72 g carbs, 16 g fiber, 2 g sugar, 1076 mg sodium

Note: *Spread guacamole only over the slices you're planning on eating, since guacamole will oxidize and turn brown on leftovers.*

Gyoza Salad

Trader Joe's Gyoza Potstickers are delicious, inexpensive, and versatile. We serve them alone as appetizers, but we also use them in soups. Here we stir-fry the potstickers with vegetables in a salad. Don't microwave these beauties. Instead, pan-fry them until they are lightly browned, then add water to steam them for a few minutes. Use any combination of crunchy vegetables, including bell peppers, onions, broccoli, or asparagus.

1 (16-oz) bag frozen vegetarian gyoza or potstickers
1 ½ cups sliced carrots
1 ½ cups sugar snap peas
¼ cup Sesame Soy Ginger Vinaigrette (more if you prefer a heavier sauce)

1   Cook gyoza according to package directions. We strongly recommend pan-frying instead of microwaving. If you choose to pan-fry, toss vegetables in with the water and steam with the gyoza. Otherwise, steam or pan-fry vegetables separately until tender-crisp.

2   Pour dressing over gyoza and vegetables. Stir until coated.

Prep and cooking time: *15 minutes*
Serves *4*

Nutrition Snapshot

Per serving: 229 calories, 3 g fat, 1 g saturated fat, 11 g protein, 39 g carbs, 4 g fiber, 9 g sugar, 628 mg sodium

Gnutmeg Gnocchi with Spinach

Gnocchi are little potato dumplings that cook up in minutes and go nicely with any combination of vegetables, cheeses, or sauces. This delicious dish features caramelized onions, fresh and colorful spinach, and crunchy walnuts. Olive oil and a splash of milk create a silky sauce accented with nutmeg and Parmesan.

1 (17.6-oz) pkg dried gnocchi
1 medium yellow onion, thinly sliced
3 Tbsp extra virgin olive oil, divided
1 clove garlic, crushed, or 1 cube frozen Crushed Garlic
¼ tsp nutmeg
⅛ tsp salt
½ cup roughly chopped walnuts (unsalted, raw or roasted)
¼ cup whole milk
1 (6-oz) bag fresh spinach (about 5-6 cups)
½ cup Parmesan cheese (shaved, shredded, or grated)

1 Cook gnocchi according to package directions.

2 In a deep skillet or wide saucepan, sauté onions in 2 Tbsp of olive oil until soft, about 5 minutes. Add garlic, nutmeg, salt, and walnuts, sautéing over low heat until onions begin to caramelize.

3 Add drained gnocchi to onion mixture and stir gently to combine. Drizzle another Tbsp of olive oil over gnocchi and add milk. Heat for an additional minute.

4 Place spinach on top, cover with a lid, and remove pan from heat. After a few minutes, once spinach has wilted down, add Parmesan and stir to combine.

Prep and cooking time: *20 minutes*
Serves *4*

Nutrition Snapshot
Per serving: 470 calories, 25 g fat, 6 g saturated fat, 14 g protein, 52 g carbs, 6 g fiber, 6 g sugar, 921 mg sodium

Helpful Tip: *Gnocchi let you know when they're cooked. When gnocchi are first placed in boiling water, they sink to the bottom. As soon as gnocchi float to the top, they're done!*

Five-Minute Shiitake Fried Rice

Sure, you can buy frozen fried rice, but why not make it yourself in about the same time and customize the ingredients to your taste? This fried rice gets its flavors from umami-rich shiitake mushrooms and the combination of ginger, garlic, and sesame in Trader Joe's Soyaki. It's ready in a snap when you use Trader Joe's frozen Jasmine Rice.

1 (10-oz) pouch frozen Organic Jasmine Rice, or 2 cups cooked rice

1 tsp olive oil

5-6 shiitake mushrooms, sliced

1½ cups frozen Organic Foursome, Soycutash, or other vegetable mix

2 Tbsp Soyaki

1 Tbsp seasoned rice vinegar

1 tsp toasted sesame oil

2 green onions, chopped or cut lengthwise

1   Heat rice according to package instructions (3 minutes in microwave).

2   Heat oil in a pan or wok over high heat and sauté mushrooms and frozen vegetables (no need to thaw) for 2 minutes until mushrooms soften.

3   Remove pan from heat and add Soyaki, vinegar, and sesame oil, stirring mixture. Add rice and stir to combine. Serve immediately, topped with green onions.

Variation: *Use your own blend of vegetables, Frozen Brown Rice instead of Jasmine, regular mushrooms instead of shiitake, add tofu, or tweak seasonings to your taste. To make this dish heartier, top with a fried or poached egg.*

Prep and cooking time: *5 minutes*
Serves *2 (or 4 as a side)*

Nutrition Snapshot
Per serving: 384 calories, 8 g fat, 1 g saturated fat, 8 g protein, 71 g carbs, 6 g fiber, 10 g sugar, 392 mg sodium

Helpful Tip: *To make green onion curly, cut it in long thin ribbons, encourage the curl by wrapping around your finger, and place in cold water. After a few minutes, the cold water will cause the green onion to curl tightly.*

Gluten Free

Substitute tamari or wheat-free soy sauce for Soyaki

Hummus and Lentil Wrap

Packaged steamed lentils make this wrap a breeze. Tasty hummus, fresh greens, and creamy yogurt complete this delicious Middle Eastern combination. The sprouted wheat tortilla has a wonderful texture and holds together nicely, making this a good wrap to take on the road.

1 Sprouted Wheat Tortilla or Lavash Bread

3 Tbsp refrigerated Mediterranean Hummus or Eggplant Hummus

5 Tbsp refrigerated Steamed Lentils

¼ cup chopped tomatoes

1 small handful Micro Greens or Herb Salad Mix

2 Tbsp yogurt, such as Plain Cream Line Yogurt

1   Place lentils, hummus, tomatoes, and micro greens down the center of the tortilla; drizzle yogurt across lentils.

2   Roll tightly.

Prep time: *5 minutes*
Serves *1*

Nutrition Snapshot

Per serving: 429 calories, 8 g fat, 2 g saturated fat, 20 g protein, 74 g carbs, 11 g fiber, 8 g sugar, 648 mg sodium

White Lightning Chili

Hearty white chili is a tomato-less alternative to traditional chili. This sweet and spicy version gets its flavor and kick from Trader Joe's well known Corn and Chile Tomato-less Salsa. Quinoa is a double-duty ingredient, thickening the chili as well as adding protein, magnesium, calcium, and iron. The quinoa will absorb most of the liquid and soften, becoming a flavorful component that binds the chili together.

½ cup uncooked quinoa, rinsed

2 cups water

1 (15-oz) can white kidney beans (cannellini beans), rinsed and drained

1 (15-oz) can pinto beans, rinsed and drained

1 (13.75-oz) jar Corn and Chile Tomato-less Salsa

1 cup Shredded Three Cheese Blend for garnish (optional)

1 Pour water into a medium or large pot. Add quinoa and bring to a boil.

2 Add remaining ingredients and return to a boil. Lower heat, cover, and simmer for 20-25 minutes, or until most of the liquid is absorbed.

3 Serve in bowls, topping with shredded cheese.

Prep time: *5 minutes*
Hands-off cooking time: *20-25 minutes*
Makes *6 (1-cup) servings*

Nutrition Snapshot
Per serving: 390 calories, 6 g fat, 2 g saturated fat, 15 g protein, 50 g carbs, 11 g fiber, 12 g sugar, 613 mg sodium

Did you know? *Quinoa cooking instructions often recommend first rinsing the quinoa. Quinoa seeds naturally have a soapy coating that can be bitter. Processing usually removes this coating, but it varies from brand to brand, so it's a good idea to give quinoa a quick rinse before using. If the water becomes slightly sudsy, then you know that the coating was there.*

G
Gluten Free

Note: *When reheating leftovers, add extra liquid, either broth or water.*

Addictive Tacos

Kerry McNaughton from Napa, California, says, "I created this recipe when I was really craving a meat taco. I wanted to make a great taco with a meat alternative that rivaled (dare I say surpassed) the tastiness of any meat taco. That night I fell in love with tacos again." We can vouch for these tacos filled with savory lentils, crunchy bell peppers, and all the fixings your heart desires. Perfect for Taco Tuesdays! For a fun variation, use lettuce instead of taco shells and make lettuce wraps.

1 (12-oz) pkg Beef-less Ground Beef or half (16-oz) bag frozen Meatless Meatballs, thawed and mashed to crumble

2 tsp olive oil

2 tsp Taco Seasoning (go easy – Trader Joe's version is much spicier than other brands)

1 cup refrigerated pre-cooked Steamed Lentils

2 cups frozen Fire Roasted Bell Peppers and Onions

12 taco shells (one 5.5-oz box) or 12 soft tortillas

½ cup yogurt or sour cream (optional)

½ cup shredded cheese (optional)

1 Heat oil in a skillet. Add Beef-less Ground Beef, taco seasoning, lentils, and veggies. Cook until heated thoroughly.

2 While filling is cooking, warm taco shells in a toaster or oven.

3 Place filling in taco shells. Serve with your choice of toppings such as yogurt, sour cream, or shredded cheese.

Prep and cook time: *10 minutes*
Makes *12 tacos*

Nutrition Snapshot
Per taco: 168 calories, 5 g fat, 1 g saturated fat, 12 g protein, 19 g carbs, 5 g fiber, 2 g sugar, 339 mg sodium

Grilled Lentil Wraps

These wraps are warm and crunchy outside and moist and savory inside. The crisp outer crust is created by toasting the tortilla in a cast iron skillet. There's no need for butter or olive oil; dry-toasting glues the seams together, so these "grilled" wraps don't fall apart like regular wraps do. Serve with your favorite chutney or salsa.

1 small onion, chopped, or 1 cup refrigerated Diced Onions

2 Tbsp olive oil

1 (10-oz) pouch frozen Organic Brown Rice, or 2 cups cooked brown rice

2 cups pre-cooked Steamed Lentils

3 cups frozen spinach (half a 16-oz bag), thawed and excess water squeezed out

¾ cup kefir or plain yogurt

1 cup shredded mozzarella cheese

6 flour tortillas

1. Heat olive oil in a skillet over medium heat. Sauté onion until soft, about 5 minutes. Meanwhile, prepare frozen rice according to package instructions. Add spinach and cook until wilted.

2. Add rice and lentils. Stir until combined and remove from heat.

3. Mix in kefir and cheese.

4. Heat ungreased griddle or skillet over medium heat. Assemble wraps by placing ⅔ cup filling in center of tortilla and folding all sides inward. Place wraps on hot skillet, seam side down. Place a bag of flour or some other heavy object on top to achieve the effect of a panini press. Toast for 3-5 minutes on each side until toasted brown and crispy.

Variations: *Use Swiss chard or any other greens instead of spinach. Substitute other types of cheese such as Havarti, Swiss, or Jack.*

Prep and cooking time: *10 minutes*
Serves *6*

Nutrition Snapshot
Per serving: 311 calories, 9 g fat, 2 g saturated fat, 13 g protein, 42 g carbs, 6 g fiber, 2 g sugar, 352 mg sodium

Spinach Ricotta Calzone

A calzone is essentially a folded pizza, traditionally stuffed with ricotta and other ingredients you would find on a pizza. This delicious variation is filled with spinach, ricotta, and sun dried tomatoes. Ready-to-use pizza dough makes it quick and easy to assemble. Top calzones with warm marinara, or put marinara in a bowl for dipping and pouring.

1 (1-lb) bag refrigerated Ready to Bake Pizza Dough
2 cups frozen chopped spinach, measured while frozen
1 cup ricotta cheese
¼ tsp salt
2 cloves garlic, crushed, or 2 cubes frozen Crushed Garlic, thawed
2 Tbsp jarred Julienne Sliced Sun Dried Tomatoes

1 Preheat oven to 450° F.

2 Divide dough in half, and roll out two 8–inch circles on a floured surface.

3 Thaw spinach. Drain, squeezing out water with your hands.

4 In a medium bowl, mix together spinach, ricotta, salt, and garlic. Stir in sun dried tomatoes. Divide the mixture between the two circles of dough, placing the mixture on half of each circle. Fold dough over into classic crescent shape and crimp edges closed with fingers or a fork. Repeat for second calzone.

5 Bake calzones on lightly oiled baking sheet or pizza stone for 20 minutes or until top is golden.

Prep time: *10 minutes*
Hands-off cooking time: *20 minutes*
Makes *2 large calzones (Serves 4)*

Nutrition Snapshot
Per half-calzone serving: 355 calories, 2g fat, 0g saturated fat, 17g protein, 61g carbs, 3g fiber, 5g sugar, 533mg sodium

My Big Fat Greek Quiche

This quiche is flavored with the classic elements of a Greek salad: spinach, feta, and tomatoes. Quiche is a versatile around-the-clock meal, appropriate at breakfast, lunch, or dinner. Serve warm or at room temperature, with a simple salad of greens, sliced cucumbers, lemon juice, and olive oil.

1 frozen pie crust, thawed

4 eggs

8 oz (½ bag) frozen chopped spinach, thawed and excess water squeezed out

1 (6-oz) container Crumbled Feta Cheese with Mediterranean Herbs

1 cup chopped tomatoes

1 cup whole milk or half-and-half

¼ tsp black pepper

⅛ tsp ground nutmeg (optional)

1   Preheat oven to 375° F.

2   Place pie crust in a 9-inch pie or quiche pan. Trim and crimp edges. Prick sides and bottom of crust with a fork.

3   Whisk together eggs, milk, pepper, and nutmeg. Add spinach, feta, and tomatoes. Stir gently to combine. Pour egg mixture into crust.

4   Bake for 40 minutes, or until knife inserted in center comes out clean.

Prep time: *10 minutes*
Hands-off cooking time: *40 minutes*
Serves *6*

Nutrition Snapshot

Per serving: 385 calories, 24 g fat, 14 g saturated fat, 15 g protein, 20 g carbs, 2 g fiber, 2 g sugar, 737 mg sodium

Gluten Free

Instead of a quiche, make a frittata. Omit the crust, preheat an oven safe skillet in a 350° F oven, and pour the filling in hot skillet. Let frittata continue cooking in oven for 30 minutes or until eggs are set.

Mozzarella and Basil Wrap

Basil, fresh mozzarella, pine nuts, and tomatoes create a fresh-from-the-garden taste. You can use pesto if you prefer, but we like the simple flavor of fresh basil in this wrap. It's delicious, and it protects your tortilla from the moisture of the cheese.

1 large (burrito size) flour tortilla

3 Fresh Mozzarella Medallions or ¼-inch-thick slices Ovoline Fresh Mozzarella

4 fresh basil leaves

3 slices Roma tomatoes or other flavorful ripe tomato

1 Tbsp toasted pine nuts

1   Lay tortilla on a flat surface. Place basil leaves down the center of the tortilla. Add mozzarella, pine nuts, and tomato.

2   Roll tightly.

Prep time: *5 minutes*
Serves *1*

Nutrition Snapshot
Per serving: 462 calories, 27 g fat, 11 g saturated fat, 23 g protein, 37 g carbs, 2 g fiber, 12 g sugar, 241 mg sodium

Arugula Pesto Pasta

Pesto – a blend of basil, nuts, Parmesan, and olive oil – is a cornerstone of Italian cooking, used generously to add flavor to a wide variety of dishes. We use Trader Joe's ready-made pesto as a dressing in this hearty pasta salad. Spicy vegetarian sausage and peppery arugula make this a great one-dish meal.

12 oz (¾ bag) whole wheat or regular penne pasta
1 (14-oz) pkg Tofurky Italian Sausage or other vegetarian sausage, sliced
1 (8-oz) container refrigerated Genova Pesto, or 1 (8-oz) jar Pesto alla Genovese
3.5 oz (½ pkg) arugula
Shredded or grated Parmesan cheese, for garnish (optional)

1   Boil pasta in salted water, according to package instructions.

2   While pasta is boiling, pan-fry sausage in lightly oiled pan. Although the sausage is fully cooked, pan-frying imparts a nicely browned color.

3   When pasta is cooked, drain. Immediately stir in pesto until noodles are coated.

4   Toss in warm sausage slices and arugula. Heat from the pasta and sausage will slightly wilt arugula.

5   Sprinkle with Parmesan cheese.

Prep and cooking time: *15 minutes*
Serves *6*

Nutrition Snapshot

Per serving: 540 calories, 26 g fat, 3 g saturated fat, 27 g protein, 50 g carbs, 6 g fiber, 2 g sugar, 425 mg sodium

G
Gluten Free

Use gluten-free pasta and omit sausage

Peanutty Sesame Noodles

These are the fresh and tasty sesame peanut noodles you remember from your favorite Chinese restaurant. Serve these flavorful noodles at room temperature or cold right out of the fridge. Add tofu chunks or sliced seitan for a boost of protein.

8 oz (half a package) spaghetti noodles
Easy Peanutty Sauce (recipe below)
1 cup shredded carrot, available pre-shredded in the produce section
1 cup sliced cucumber
2 green onions, chopped
¼ cup roasted peanuts, crushed

1 Cook noodles according to package directions. Drain.

2 Pour Easy Peanutty Sauce over noodles and toss until noodles are evenly coated. Add carrots and cucumber. Toss gently.

3 Top with green onions and crushed peanuts.

Easy Peanutty Sauce
¼ cup Soyaki or Veri Veri Teriyaki
¼ cup creamy salted peanut butter
2 Tbsp toasted sesame oil
¼ cup water

1 Whisk Soyaki, peanut butter, and sesame oil until blended.

2 Add water and mix well.

Prep time: *10 minutes*
Hands-off cooking time: *10 minutes*
Serves 6

Nutrition Snapshot
Per serving: 463 calories, 22 g fat, 3 g saturated fat, 15 g protein, 55 g carbs, 8 g fiber, 9 g sugar, 526 mg sodium

Roasted Asparagus with
    Tomatoes and Feta **165**

Black Bean Cornbread **166**

Eggplant Zucchini Bake **167**

Crunchy Broccoli Slaw **169**

Balsamic Roasted Fennel **170**

Coconut Curried Vegetables **171**

Oven Roasted Vegetables with Rosemary **172**

Baked Sweet Potato Fries **174**

Roasted Cauliflower with Olives **177**

Loco for Coconut Rice **178**

Pan-Toasted Brussels Sprouts **181**

Couscous with Sun Dried Tomatoes **182**

Sesame Toasted Sugar Snap Peas **185**

Almond Bread **187**

Sides

Roasted Asparagus with Tomatoes and Feta

Dress up asparagus with ripe tomatoes and savory feta cheese. Unlike steaming, which can yield a stringy washed-out vegetable, roasting preserves the fresh green color and crisp texture of asparagus. This colorful dish is an elegant accompaniment to any meal, especially one with a Mediterranean or Greek theme.

1 (12-oz) pkg fresh asparagus spears
2 tsp olive oil
⅛ tsp salt
1 tomato, sliced
1 Tbsp Crumbled Feta
⅛ tsp black pepper

1   Preheat oven to 400° F.

2   On baking sheet, toss asparagus with oil until well coated. Line up asparagus in a single layer, sides touching. Sprinkle lightly with salt.

3   Place sliced tomatoes in a row along the center. Sprinkle feta cheese and pepper evenly on top.

4   Bake for 10 minutes until asparagus is crisp-tender. For softer asparagus, cook 5-10 minutes longer.

Prep time: *10 minutes*
Hands-off cooking time: *15 minutes*
Serves *6 (about 3 spears per person)*

Nutrition Snapshot
Per serving: 42 calories, 3 g fat, 1 g saturated fat, 2 g protein, 4 g carbs, 2 g fiber, 2 g sugar, 71 mg sodium

G
Gluten Free

Black Bean Cornbread

Trader Joe's Cornbread Mix is a sweet cornbread, which may come as a surprise to Southerners who enjoy it salty. Here we have created a sweet and savory version by adding a can of Organic Black Bean Soup. The beans and added corn, onion, and tomato make for a hearty bread. It's perfect paired with a simple soup or chowder. (Check out Trader Joe's wide selection of ready-to-go boxed soups.) Now here's the bonus: each piece of cornbread has only ½ gram of fat and more than 5 grams of protein.

1 box Cornbread Mix
2 egg whites
1 (14.5-oz) can Organic Black Bean Soup
½ cup 2% or whole milk

1   Preheat oven to 350° F.

2   Beat together egg whites, soup, and milk.

3   Stir in dry cornbread mix. Don't add any of the other ingredients called for on box instructions.

4   Pour into oiled 8 x 8 x 2-inch baking pan and bake for 35-40 minutes or until a toothpick inserted in cornbread comes out clean.

Prep time: *5 minutes,* **Hands-off cooking time:** *35-40 minutes,* **Serves** *9*

Nutrition Snapshot
Per piece: 202 calories, 0.5 g fat, 0 g saturated fat, 5 g protein, 43 g carbs, 2 g fiber, 17 g sugar, 338 mg sodium

Eggplant Zucchini Bake

This side dish uses one of our favorites at Trader Joe's, refrigerated Fresh Bruschetta Sauce. The intense flavors of the sauce complement the simple combination of eggplant and zucchini. After baking, the bread crumbs get crisp, the zucchini tender (but not mushy), and the eggplant softened and silky.

1 medium eggplant
4 medium zucchini
1 Tbsp extra virgin olive oil
1 (8-oz) container refrigerated Fresh Bruschetta Sauce
½ cup bread crumbs

1 Preheat oven to 400° F.

2 Peel and slice eggplant into (slightly thicker than) ¼-inch slices crosswise.

3 Slice zucchini lengthwise into ½-inch slices.

4 Coat bottom of an 8x12 or 9x13-inch baking pan with olive oil. Arrange eggplant slices on the bottom, and top with zucchini slices.

5 Pour bruschetta sauce evenly over the dish.

6 Sprinkle bread crumbs on top and bake for about 40 minutes.

Prep time: *10 minutes,* **Hands-off cooking time:** *40 minutes,* **Serves** *6*

Nutrition Snapshot
Per serving: 141 calories, 8 g fat, 1 g saturated fat, 4 g protein, 18g carbs, 4 g fiber, 7 g sugar, 244 mg sodium

Crunchy Broccoli Slaw

This interesting twist on traditional coleslaw calls for shredded broccoli instead of cabbage. The suggested dressings are all good alternatives to the traditional (high fat and calorie) mayonnaise dressing. For a homemade dressing, mix two parts extra virgin olive oil with one part balsamic vinegar whisked with a dollop of Dijon mustard.

1 (12-oz) bag Organic Broccoli Slaw, or 5 cups shredded broccoli and carrots
½ cup Tuscan Italian Vinaigrette or Sweet Poppyseed Dressing (if you like sweeter dressings)
⅓ cup sliced green onion (2 stalks)
½ cup raw sunflower seeds
½ cup slivered almonds

1   Combine dressing and slaw. Toss until evenly distributed.

2   Add remaining ingredients and combine.

3   Chill and serve.

Variation: *For an Asian-inspired slaw, use Sesame Soy Ginger Vinaigrette (fat free).*

Prep time: *5 minutes*
Serves *8*

Nutrition Snapshot

Per serving: 109 calories, 8 g fat, 1 g saturated fat, 5 g protein, 6 g carbs, 2 g fiber, 0 g sugar, 275 mg sodium

Balsamic Roasted Fennel

The fennel bulb is the thick base of fennel stalk and is packed with antioxidants and other nutrients. Roasted fennel slices are tender, delicious, and gorgeously caramelized and browned on the edges. Roasting brings out the nutty flavor of fennel and is a perfect addition to a fall or holiday meal.

1.25 lbs fennel bulbs (2 fist-sized fennel bulbs)
2 Tbsp extra virgin olive oil
2 Tbsp Balsamic vinegar
Pinch salt and pepper
Parmesan cheese (optional)

1 Preheat oven to 400° F.

2 Slice bulbs into ½-inch-thick slices.

3 Place bulbs on a baking sheet (optionally lined with a Silpat baking mat) and drizzle with olive oil and balsamic vinegar. Toss to coat the slices. Sprinkle with salt and pepper.

4 Place in oven and roast for 45 minutes, flipping the slices halfway through cooking time.

5 When serving, sprinkle with Parmesan.

Prep time: *5 minutes,* **Hands-off cooking time:** *45 minutes,* **Serves** *4*

Nutrition Snapshot
Per serving: 104 calories, 7 g fat, 1 g saturated fat, 2g protein, 10 g carbs, 4 g fiber, 1 g sugar, 99 mg sodium

Gluten Free

Coconut Curried Vegetables

Coconut milk simmers down to a creamy sauce for the vegetables in this dish. You can substitute other vegetables, such as cauliflower, green beans, or peas. Serve with any Indian or Southeast Asian entrée.

3 zucchini, sliced into ½-inch or 1-inch pieces
2 carrots, chopped or cut lengthwise into thin pieces
1 red bell pepper, cut into 1-inch pieces
1 cup Light Coconut Milk (half the can)
1 tsp curry powder
1 clove garlic, crushed, or 1 cube frozen Crushed Garlic
½ tsp salt

1 In a deep skillet or wide saucepan, combine coconut milk, curry powder, garlic, and salt.

2 Bring sauce to a simmer and add vegetables. Simmer for about 10-15 minutes until vegetables are tender.

Prep time: 5-10 minutes, **Hands-off cooking time**: 10-15 minutes, **Serves** 4

Nutrition Snapshot
Per serving: 82 calories, 3 g fat, 2 g saturated fat, 2 g protein, 13 g carbs, 4 g fiber, 5 g sugar, 354 mg sodium

Oven Roasted Vegetables with Rosemary

Your kitchen is going to smell great as you roast vegetables with garlic and fresh rosemary. This healthy selection of squash, sweet potato, and red pepper is a nice accompaniment to nearly any entrée. The conveniently prepped bagged vegetables make this dish a breeze without all the peeling and chopping. Keep leftovers for use in wraps or sandwiches the next day!

2 zucchini, sliced thinly lengthwise (¼-inch thick or less)

1 cup cut butternut squash (available bagged)

1 cup cut yams (available bagged)

1 red bell pepper, quartered, with seeds and pith removed

6-8 garlic cloves, peeled

3 Tbsp extra virgin olive oil

½ tsp salt

¼ tsp pepper

A few sprigs fresh rosemary

1   Preheat oven to 425° F.

2   Toss vegetables with olive oil, salt, and pepper, thoroughly coating all vegetables.

3   Place vegetables in a single layer in a 9 x 13-inch roasting/baking pan. Make sure red peppers are cut side down. Place pan in the oven and roast uncovered for 20 minutes.

4   Add rosemary and roast for an additional 10-15 minutes or until veggies look done.

Prep time: *10 minutes*
Hands-off cooking time: *35 minutes*
Serves *6*

Nutrition Snapshot

Per serving: 122 calories, 7 g fat, 1 g saturated fat, 2 g protein, 15 g carbs, 3 g fiber, 3 g sugar, 178 mg sodium

Baked Sweet Potato Fries

Fries are irresistible, and this lean version of the deep-fried variety is guilt-free. While not quite as crispy as classic French fries, these are packed with more flavor, thanks to the sweet potatoes. These are so popular at our house, we always double the recipe (in which case, use two baking sheets).

1 (12-oz) bag pre-cut Sweet Potato Spears
1 Tbsp olive oil
¼ tsp salt
¼ tsp curry powder or ground cumin (optional)

1 Preheat oven to 400° F.

2 Toss sweet potatoes with olive oil, until spears are evenly coated. Sprinkle with salt and curry, and mix again.

3 Spread spears in a single layer on a baking sheet. Bake for 20-30 minutes until cooked, stirring halfway through cooking for best results.

4 Serve immediately. Baked fries get soggy quickly.

Variation: *For garlic fries: use 1 tsp crushed garlic or ½ tsp garlic powder instead of curry powder. Sprinkle with chopped parsley just before serving.*

Prep time: *5 minutes*
Hands-off cooking time: *20-30 minutes*
Serves *4*

Nutrition Snapshot
Per serving: 90 calories, 3 g fat, 0 g saturated fat, 1 g protein, 15 g carbs, 3 g fiber, 3 g sugar, 155 mg sodium

G
Gluten Free

Roasted Cauliflower with Olives

It was common decades ago to boil the life out of cauliflower, leaving it mushy and tasteless. Enter the new age of roasted cauliflower – a simple and incredibly delicious dish that will forever change the way you think about this vegetable. Roasting at high heat brings out cauliflower's natural sweetness, balanced here by salty Kalamata olives. If you skip the olives, sprinkle cauliflower lightly with salt, or add grated Parmesan cheese after roasting. This is a rustic dish that's equally good as an appetizer or side.

1 (12-oz) pkg Cauliflower Florets, or 4 cups cauliflower cut into florets
4 tsp olive oil
½ tsp 21 Seasoning Salute, or your favorite seasoning
½ cup Kalamata olives, about a dozen

1 Preheat oven to 400° F.

2 Toss cauliflower with olive oil. Sprinkle with seasoning and stir to coat. Mix in olives.

3 Place cauliflower mixture on baking sheet, spreading in a single layer. Roast for 20 minutes, flipping halfway through baking time to roast evenly. Cauliflower will be crisp-tender. For softer cauliflower, continue roasting for an additional 10 minutes.

Prep time: *5 minutes*
Hands-off cooking time: *20 minutes*
Serves *6*

Nutrition Snapshot
Per serving: 58 calories, 4 g fat, 1 g saturated fat, 2 g protein, 5 g carbs, 2 g fiber, 2 g sugar, 381 mg sodium

G Gluten Free

Loco for Coconut Rice

Enjoy this delicate coconut rice with Thai dishes or Indian curries. Coconut milk gives ordinary rice a hint of exotic flavor and a creamy and silky texture without a lot of added fat and calories. Add extra coconut milk near the end of cooking time to achieve a creamy risotto-like texture.

1 cup jasmine rice
1 cup water
1 cup light coconut milk
¼ tsp salt

1   In a medium saucepan, combine rice, water, coconut milk, and salt.

2   Bring mixture to a boil. Reduce heat and cover, simmering 15 minutes, or until all water is absorbed. Remove from heat and allow to rest for 5 minutes, then fluff with fork.

Prep time: *2 minutes*
Hands-off cooking time: *20 minutes*
Serves *4*

Nutrition Snapshot
Per serving: 210 calories, 3 g fat, 2 g saturated fat, 3 g protein, 41 g carbs, 0 g fiber, 1 g sugar, 163 mg sodium

G
Gluten Free

Pan-Toasted Brussels Sprouts

Who hasn't eaten a Brussels sprout and pretended to be a giant eating an entire head of cabbage in one bite? Vegetable broth steams and flavors the Brussels sprouts, making them ready in a hurry in this fabulous pan-fried recipe. The Guinness record for eating Brussels sprouts is 44 in one minute. Try our recipe and you might be a contender.

1 (12-oz) pkg Brussels sprouts
2 tsp olive oil or butter
½ cup vegetable broth or water (add heavy pinch of salt if using water)
Grated or shredded Parmesan cheese (optional)

1 Heat olive oil in saucepan over medium heat.

2 Cut Brussels sprouts in half. Place them cut-side down in hot pan. Add broth. When broth comes to a boil, cover and cook for 5 minutes.

3 Remove lid and continue to cook until broth evaporates and Brussels sprouts are browned.

4 Remove from heat and sprinkle with Parmesan cheese.

Prep and cooking time: *10 minutes*
Serves *4*

Nutrition Snapshot
Per serving: 63 calories, 3 g fat, 0 g saturated fat, 2 g protein, 6 g carbs, 3 g fiber, 2 g sugar, 97 mg sodium

Use gluten-free broth

Couscous with Sun Dried Tomatoes

The flavors of Tuscany come alive with this easy dish. Couscous is a terrific side dish because it takes only minutes to prepare and easily replaces rice or pasta. Marinated artichokes and sun dried tomatoes add a sweet and savory flavor and are easy pantry items to keep on hand. Add any combination of fresh herbs or even goat cheese or feta.

1½ cups dry Whole Wheat Couscous
1 (12-oz) jar Marinated Artichokes; do not drain
½ (8.5-oz) jar Julienne Sliced Sun Dried Tomatoes, drained completely
1 cup water
¼ cup chopped fresh basil

1 Pour liquid from jar of artichokes into a medium saucepan. Roughly chop artichokes.

2 To the saucepan, add chopped artichokes, tomatoes, and water. Bring to a boil.

3 Stir in couscous, remove pan from heat, and cover for 5 minutes until water is absorbed. Fluff, stir in basil, and serve.

Prep and cooking time: *10 minutes*
Serves *6*

Nutrition Snapshot

Per serving: 282 calories, 10 g fat, 1 g saturated fat, 8 g protein, 41 g carbs, 5 g fiber, 1 g sugar, 381 mg sodium

Sesame Toasted Sugar Snap Peas

Sugar snap peas are delicious on their own and can be eaten raw. The less you do to them, the better, to let their crunchy sweet taste shine. Here we make the peas glisten with just a smidge of nutty sesame oil. A quick burst of heat enhances their naturally sweet flavor and vibrant color. Do not overcook.

1 (12-oz) bag Sugar Snap Peas or snow peas
1 tsp toasted sesame oil
Pinch salt
2 Tbsp water
1 tsp sesame seeds

1 Heat skillet or wok over medium-high heat.

2 Mix peas, sesame oil, and salt in a mixing bowl until evenly coated.

3 Toss peas into skillet. Add water and quickly stir-fry for 2-3 minutes until water evaporates and peas are bright green and still crisp.

4 Remove from heat and sprinkle with sesame seeds.

Prep and cooking time: *5 minutes*
Serves *4*

Nutrition Snapshot
Per serving: 49 calories, 2 g fat, 0 g saturated fat, 2 g protein, 6 g carbs, 2 g fiber, 3 g sugar, 39 mg sodium

G *Gluten Free*

Almond Bread

Almond meal is a slightly more coarse version of almond flour, made of ground almonds with the skin left on. We use it to make delicious and healthy almond bread that is low carb, high protein, and gluten free. This bread was inspired by a recipe from Elana Amsterdam at the Elana's Pantry blog. We love the nutty taste and moist, hearty texture. Enjoy plain or topped with cream cheese and honey.

1 (16-oz) bag almond meal (about 4½ cups)
1 tsp salt
1 tsp baking soda
1 Tbsp baking powder
5 large eggs
2 Tbsp agave nectar
½ cup plain yogurt such as Plain Cream Line Yogurt
1 tsp sesame seeds (optional)

1. Preheat oven to 325° F.
2. In a large bowl, combine almond meal, salt, baking soda, and baking powder.
3. In a medium bowl, whisk together eggs, agave nectar, and yogurt.
4. Add wet mixture to dry mixture and mix thoroughly.
5. Pour mixture into a 5 x 9-inch oiled loaf pan and sprinkle with sesame seeds.
6. Immediately place in oven on center rack and bake for 55 minutes, or until a toothpick inserted in center comes out clean. If top begins to brown too much, drape with foil. When cool, run a sharp knife along edge of pan to loosen bread and remove to slice.

Prep time: *10 minutes*
Hands-off cooking time: *55 minutes*
Serves *12*

Nutrition Snapshot
Per serving: 317 calories, 25 g fat, 2 g saturated fat, 13 g protein, 11 g carbs, 5 g fiber, 2 g sugar, 450 mg sodium

Gluten Free

Honey, I Ate the Chocolate
     Bread Pudding **191**

Low-Fat Wide Awake Coffee Shake **192**

Lemon Basil Cake **193**

Monkey Bread **194**

Chocolate Truffle Pie with Joe-Joe's Crust **197**

All Mixed Up Margaritas **198**

Chocolate Lava Cake **200**

Chia Energy Drink (Chia Fresca) **203**

One Bowl Peach & Blueberry Cobbler **204**

Simple Apple Tart **207**

Orange Creamsicle Smoothie **208**

Very Berry Mascarpone Tart **210**

Lemon Drop Martini **213**

No Moo Mousse **214**

Good-for-you Strawberries and Cream **216**

Mango Lassi **217**

Frozen Tiramisu **218**

Almond Pudding **221**

Nearly Instant Homemade Mango Ice Cream **222**

Vanilla Chai Bread Pudding **225**

Lemon Tart with Fresh Berries **226**

Peachy Sangria **227**

Chocolate Coffee Fudge **229**

"A Hint of Coffee" Brownies with Café Latte Glaze **230**

Mighty Mojito **233**

Desserts & Drinks

Honey, I Ate the Chocolate Bread Pudding

Cold vanilla ice cream melting on warm bread pudding is one of those feel-good dessert combinations. And this recipe makes a happy cook as well. There's no melting butter, no measuring ingredients: just toss it all in and bake. We justify our chocolate indulgence by claiming this pudding is healthy since we use whole wheat ingredients! Serve warm with vanilla ice cream. Or, if you really want to be indulgent (and we encourage it), serve with chocolate ice cream.

½ **loaf (8 slices) Whole Wheat Honey Bread**
1 ½ **cups Brownie Truffle Baking Mix (just the dry mix, don't add anything else)**
2 ½ **cups whole milk**

1   Cut crusts off bread slices. Cube bread into ½-inch by ½-inch pieces. Toss diced bread in an 8 x 8-inch lightly greased or buttered baking pan and arrange so pan is filled evenly.

2   Combine milk and brownie mix. Stir well for a minute until dissolved. Pour brownie mixture over diced bread. Lightly press down on bread pieces so that they are thoroughly soaked through with brownie liquid.

3   Set pan aside while you preheat oven to 350° F, perhaps 10 minutes or so. This extra time will give the bread time to soak further. Cover pan tightly with foil and bake for 30 minutes.

4   When done, remove pan from oven and let it cool for 15 minutes, allowing bread pudding to set. Serve warm.

Prep time: *5-10 minutes*
Hands-off cooking time: *30 minutes*
Serves *9*

Nutrition Snapshot
Per serving: 272 calories, 5 g fat,
3 g saturated fat, 7 g protein,
56 g carbs, 4 g fiber, 29 g sugar, 201 mg sodium

Low-Fat Wide Awake Coffee Shake

Love coffee? This low-fat version of a thick coffee shake uses nonfat plain frozen yogurt – deliciously tangy and not too sweet. Chocolate covered espresso beans add sweet crunch and an intense burst of coffee and chocolate flavor. Similar shakes typically use vanilla or coffee ice cream, which has a whopping 600+ calories per 1-cup serving, half of which are fat calories. The nonfat frozen yogurt used in this recipe has ⅓ the calories and zero fat, making it a guiltless treat.

2 cups Nonfat Plain Frozen Yogurt

⅓ cup water with 1 Tbsp instant coffee dissolved in it, or ⅓ cup cold strong coffee

12 Dark Chocolate Covered Espresso Beans (about ¼ cup)

1   Combine all ingredients in a blender and blend until smooth. Adjust the amount of liquid to get the consistency you like.

2   Pour into tall glasses and serve immediately.

Prep time: *5 minutes,* **Serves** *2*

Nutrition Snapshot

Per serving: 265 calories, 2 g fat, 1 g saturated fat, 9 g protein, 52 g carbs, 0 g fiber, 45 g sugar, 121 mg sodium

Gluten Free

Lemon Basil Cake

Western dessert recipes routinely call for spices like cinnamon and nutmeg, but herbs have not been as popular. Lately, however, herbs are popping up in sweet desserts everywhere, including rosemary cake, basil sherbet, and lavender custard. Lemon and basil combine deliciously to turn ordinary vanilla cake into something unique and flavorful.

1 pkg Vanilla Cake & Baking Mix (requires 2 eggs, 1 stick melted butter or ½ cup oil, and 1 cup cold milk)

Zest of 2 lemons, about 2 Tbsp (use a lemon zester to make it easy)

½ cup finely chopped fresh basil

Blueberries or whipped cream (optional)

1 Preheat oven to 350° F.

2 Mix together cake batter as directed. When the batter is smooth, stir in lemon zest and basil.

3 Spread batter in oiled 8x8-inch pan. Bake 40-43 minutes or until toothpick inserted in center comes out clean.

4 Cool and remove from pan. When serving slices, top with blueberries or whipped cream.

Prep time: *5-10 minutes,* Hands-off cooking time: *40 minutes,* Serves *9*

Nutrition Snapshot
Per serving: 312 calories, 13 g fat, 7 g saturated fat, 5 g protein, 45 g carbs, 1 g fiber, 26 g sugar, 438 mg sodium

Monkey Bread

Yes, it's so 1960s, but it's so darn good. This lazy version of cinnamon rolls is often served for brunch but is decadent enough to qualify as dessert. Monkey bread is a yummy gooey pastry that makes no pretense about being a diet food. It is usually made with dough that needs to rise before baking. Our version uses buttermilk biscuits, which can be baked right away. It is infinitely better when enjoyed warm, straight out of the oven.

2 (16-oz) cans refrigerated Buttermilk Biscuits
½ cup white sugar
2 tsp cinnamon
6 Tbsp butter
½ cup brown sugar
2 Tbsp maple syrup
⅓ cup chopped nuts (optional)
¼ cup raisins (optional)

1   Preheat oven to 350° F.

2   Mix white sugar and cinnamon in a large bowl. Cut biscuits into fourths and toss biscuit pieces in cinnamon sugar until each piece is coated.

3   If using nuts and raisins, sprinkle several spoonfuls into the bottom of a Bundt pan. Arrange biscuit pieces in pan, sprinkling remaining nuts and raisins as you go along. Pour any remaining cinnamon sugar into pan.

4   Melt butter and brown sugar in a small saucepan, stirring until dissolved. Remove from heat and stir in maple syrup. Pour this mixture evenly over biscuits.

5   Bake for 35-40 minutes, or until browned. Invert immediately onto a serving plate, letting the sticky syrup pour out (otherwise syrup will harden on bottom of pan). Serve immediately.

Prep time: *15 minutes*
Hands-off cooking time: *35-40 minutes*
Serves *12*

Nutrition Snapshot

Per serving (not including nuts or raisins): 302 calories, 8 g fat, 4 g saturated fat, 5 g protein, 54 g carbs, 1 g fiber, 24 g sugar, 669 mg sodium

Note: *If you don't have a Bundt pan, use a 9 x13-inch pan, or halve the recipe and bake in an 8- or 9-inch round pan, reducing cooking time to ~25 minutes.*

About: *Joe-Joe's cookies are Trader Joe's version of classic Oreos, with either a vanilla bean filling or chocolate filling. They have all natural flavoring and no hydrogenated oils. You know the holidays are here when Candy Cane Joe Joe's make their limited appearance on shelves and cause Trader Joe's fans to stampede down the aisles. You know who you are.*

Chocolate Truffle Pie with Joe-Joe's Crust

The votes are in. Deana's two young kids announced, "Mom, this is the best dessert you've ever made." It might also be the easiest. The chocolate filling is firm and silky, and uses only two ingredients. The chocolate crust is easy and made with crushed Trader Joe's Joe-Joe's cookies.

Crust
28 Joe-Joe's Cookies with Vanilla Bean filling (2 rows out of the package)
¼ cup melted unsalted butter

Filling
1 (12-oz) bag semi-sweet chocolate chips
1 (14-oz) can light coconut milk

1   Preheat oven to 350° F.

2   Crush cookies in a food processor. Pulse until cookies are fine crumbs. Pour in melted butter and pulse until combined. Press crumbs firmly into an oven-safe pie dish and up the sides, using the bottom of a glass or a measuring cup to apply pressure and form crust.

3   Bake crust for 5 minutes. Remove from oven and cool completely.

4   Melt chocolate, either on stovetop or in microwave. (Microwave method: Place chips in a small glass bowl and microwave for 1 minute and then in 30 second increments, stirring well in between until completely smooth and melted. Do not scorch.)

5   Pour coconut milk into a blender and add melted chocolate. Blend immediately, until mixture is completely smooth, about 20-30 seconds.

6   Pour filling into crust and chill for 4 hours or overnight in fridge.

Prep and cooking time: *15-20 minutes, not including cooling/chilling time*
Serves *12*

Nutrition Snapshot
Per serving: 341 calories, 21 g fat, 10 g saturated fat, 2 g protein, 3 g carbs, 2 g fiber, 29 g sugar, 155 mg sodium

All Mixed Up Margaritas

Trader Joe's has a great Margarita Mix, but perhaps you're feeling a little more adventurous. Instead of a mix, try some of the juices we suggest below: pomegranate, pink lemonade, or sparkling lime soda to name a few. There's no substitute for fresh lime in an authentic-tasting margarita, so have plenty on hand. Most importantly, make sure to pick up a real lime squeezer so your friends will believe you when you claim to be a Margarita master.

¼ cup juice (Organic Pink Lemonade, French Market Limeade, or Just Pomegranate)
½ oz (1 Tbsp) Triple Sec or other orange-flavored liqueur
2 oz (4 Tbsp) tequila (we like Tequila Reserva 1800 Reposado)
2 Tbsp lime juice (juice of 1 lime)
Ice cubes or crushed ice

1   If you want to salt the rim, rub the rim with a cut lime and dip in a shallow dish of kosher or flaked salt. It's also fun using different kinds of sugar to "salt" the rim (such as Turbinado Sugar with the pomegranate version, or Organic Sugar with the Pink Lemonade version).

2   Add ingredients to a glass cup. Add enough ice to fill remainder of cup and stir.

For a small pitcher
1 cup juice (or 1 ½ cups if you don't want it too strong)
¼ cup Triple Sec
1 cup tequila
½ cup lime juice (juice of 4 limes)
3 cups ice

Prep time: *5 minutes*
Serves *1 (pitcher serves 4)*

Nutrition Snapshot
Per serving: 218 calories, 0 g fat, 0 g saturated fat, 0 g protein, 16 g carbs, 0 g fiber, 13 g sugar, 0 mg sodium

Gluten Free

Chocolate Lava Cake

Chocolate Lava Cake is a brownie-like cake with a warm pudding center that oozes out when cut. For chocolate lovers, this is heaven on a plate. It's been said this cake was invented by mistake when a baker forgot to put flour in the cake batter. We think it's one of the best mistakes in baking history. Although Trader Joe's sells ready-made frozen chocolate lava cake, this homemade version adapted from Jean-George Vongerichten's classic is superior, and it really doesn't take much effort. Serve with fresh fruit or vanilla ice cream.

½ cup (1 stick) butter, plus extra for buttering the molds
4 oz dark/bittersweet chocolate, preferably Valrhona**
2 eggs
2 egg yolks
¼ cup sugar
1 tsp instant coffee, dissolved in ½ tsp hot water (optional)
2 Tbsp flour, plus a little more for dusting the molds
Powdered sugar for garnish (optional)
Four (4-oz) ramekins or molds

1   Preheat oven to 450° F.

2   Break up chocolate into pieces in a glass mixing bowl. Cut up butter into chunks and add to chocolate. Melt chocolate and butter over a double-boiler or in the microwave (use 30-second intervals, stirring in between) until chocolate is melted. Whisk to combine.

3   Whisk eggs, egg yolks, sugar, and coffee in a small bowl. Pour egg mixture into melted chocolate and stir well. Add flour and stir just until combined. Do not overmix.

4   Butter ramekins and dust with flour, shaking out excess. Divide batter evenly among molds.

5   Place ramekins on a baking tray and bake for 6-7 minutes, or until sides are set. The center will be soft and look undercooked (see photo on next page).

6   Wait for 10 seconds before inverting molds onto serving dishes. After inverting, sprinkle lightly with powdered sugar. Serve immediately.

Prep and cooking time: *15-20 minutes*
Serves *4*

**Valrhona is widely acknowledged as the premium chocolate bar for bakers. If you're making this dessert for a large crowd, Trader Joe's Pound Plus dark chocolate is an acceptable substitute and offers a great value.*

Nutrition Snapshot

Per serving (not including garnish): 508 calories, 40 g fat, 23 g saturated fat, 8 g protein, 8 g carbs, 10 g fiber, 13 g sugar, 48 mg sodium

Cake is done when sides are set and center is still soft

Helpful Tip: *To invert molds, run a knife along sides to loosen cake. Place serving plate over mold. Using oven mitts, hold plate firmly against mold and quickly invert. Lightly tap mold until cake releases. Remove mold and serve.*

Chia Energy Drink (Chia Fresca)

Whole chia seeds are combined with fresh lime juice, sugar, and water to create a chia energy drink. This ancient seed and superfood is high in protein, omega-3 fatty acids, fiber, and vitamins. The recipe was inspired by the book *Born to Run* in which *chia fresca* sustains the Tarahumara running people on their many-hundred-mile runs. Deana's husband swears by this drink ever since he started using chia before his triathlons and century-long bike rides. Whether you're an athlete, an Aztec warrior fueling up for battle, or just someone looking for a health boost, this drink is a delicious and easy way to add chia to your diet.

2 Tbsp whole chia seeds

2 cups water

4 Tbsp fresh lime juice

2 Tbsp sugar (or honey or agave to taste)

1   Combine ingredients in a Mason jar or small pitcher and stir until sugar is dissolved and chia is distributed in water. Chia may clump at first, so use a whisk if necessary. Taste and adjust sugar and lime juice as needed—it should have the sweet and sour balance of limeade or lemonade.

2   Allow drink to sit for 20-30 minutes or overnight in fridge until chia seeds have softened and the liquid is like a thin gel.

3   Store in fridge. Shake jar or stir as needed to re-suspend chia seeds in the liquid.

Prep time: *5 minutes*
Serves *2*

Nutrition Snapshot

Per serving: 112 calories, 3g fat, 0g saturated fat, 3g protein, 19g carbs, 5g fiber, 13g sugar, 1mg sodium

Gluten Free

One Bowl Peach & Blueberry Cobbler

This may be the easiest cobbler you can make. Simply throw all the ingredients in an oven-safe dish and top with any fruit you have on hand. The result is warm fruit comfortably nestled in soft pillows of dough. Serve with whipped cream or a scoop of vanilla ice cream.

1 cup Buttermilk Pancake Mix

¼ cup butter, melted

½ cup sugar

½ cup milk

3 cups sliced peaches (fresh, frozen, or canned, such as jarred Peaches in Light Syrup) thawed and drained if using frozen

½ cup blueberries, fresh or frozen

¼ tsp ground cinnamon (optional)

1 Preheat oven to 375° F.

2 Select an 8 x 8-inch square ovenproof dish or a glass 9-inch pie plate for the cobbler. (If you're feeding a crowd, double the recipe and use a 9 x13-inch baking dish.) Melt butter right in the baking dish and use it as a mixing bowl.

3 Add pancake mix, sugar, and milk to melted butter. Stir with a fork until just combined. Batter will be lumpy – do not over mix.

4 Scatter peaches and blueberries evenly over batter. Lightly sprinkle cinnamon evenly on top.

5 Bake for 30 minutes or until light golden brown.

Variations: *Use apples, pears, plums, or mixed berries. Frozen and canned fruit work just as well as fresh fruit in this recipe, but be sure to thaw and drain first.*

Prep time: *5 minutes*
Hands-off cooking time: *30 minutes*
Serves *4*

Nutrition Snapshot

Per serving: 389 calories, 14 g fat, 8 g saturated fat, 6 g protein, 63 g carbs, 3 g fiber, 42 g sugar, 469 mg sodium

Simple Apple Tart

A remarkably beautiful tart, irresistible in its simplicity and absolutely delicious! There are only four ingredients for this sophisticated version of apple pie. For a fancy touch, warm some apricot jam (to make it easier to spread) and brush on top of cooked tart. The jam will make the apples glisten.

1 pie crust, thawed if frozen
4 large or 5 medium Golden Delicious apples
2 Tbsp sugar
2 Tbsp unsalted butter, sliced thin
2 Tbsp apricot jam, warmed (optional)

1   Preheat oven to 350° F.

2   Press pie crust into a 10-inch tart pan. Trim any excess crust. Prick evenly with a fork.

3   Peel, core, and thinly slice apples (about 1/8-inch thick). Arrange in overlapping pattern on pie crust.

4   Sprinkle sugar evenly over apples. Spread butter pieces evenly over apples.

5   Bake for 45 minutes or until apples are golden. Glaze tart by brushing with warm apricot jam.

Prep time: *20 minutes*
Hands-off cooking time: *45 minutes*
Serves *8*

Nutrition Snapshot
Per serving: 267 calories, 16g fat, 9g saturated fat, 2g protein, 31g carbs, 4g fiber, 5g sugar, 46mg sodium

Orange Creamsicle Smoothie

Remember those yummy orange Creamsicles we all loved as kids? This creamy smoothie captures the orange and vanilla essence of those beloved popsicles in a healthy morning smoothie. If you don't like using ice in smoothies, or if your blender can't blend ice, simply substitute a second cup of mango for the cup of ice.

1 cup Vanilla Nonfat Yogurt
1 cup orange juice
1 cup frozen Mango Chunks
1 cup crushed ice
1 tsp vanilla

1   Add all ingredients to blender and blend until smooth.
2   Pour into glasses and garnish with an orange slice.

Prep time: *5 minutes*
Makes *2 (1½-cup) servings*

Nutrition Snapshot
Per serving: 172 calories, 0 g fat, 0 g saturated fat, 6 g protein, 36 g carbs, 2 g fiber, 30 g sugar, 52 mg sodium

Gluten Free

Very Berry Mascarpone Tart

This delightful dessert is a great use of mascarpone cheese, the Italian version of cream cheese. We like the rustic look of colorful berries piled up in no particular order, but you could arrange the berries in a symmetrical pattern too. You can skip the crust and make a parfait version by layering the filling and berries in a glass. Substitute any fresh fruit you like, such as peaches or figs. Just be sure the fruit is ripe and in season for optimum flavor.

1 frozen pie crust, thawed
½ cup heavy whipping cream
¼ cup sugar
1 (8-oz) container mascarpone cheese, softened at room temperature
Pinch salt
1 Tbsp finely grated lemon zest (optional)
1 pint each: fresh raspberries, blueberries, blackberries

1 Preheat oven to 450° F. Don't forget to let mascarpone cheese soften at room temperature.

2 Press pie crust into a 10-inch tart pan or regular pie pan and cut off excess crust. Prick crust in several places with a fork. For a perfectly shaped crust, place wax paper on top of crust and fill with raw beans or rice. Bake for 15 minutes; remove wax paper and bake 5 minutes longer or until golden brown. If you don't mind more casual-looking crust that may sag in places, simply bake unfilled for 10 minutes. Let crust cool completely.

3 Using an electric mixer, beat heavy cream and sugar until stiff peaks form. Be careful not to over-mix. Stir in mascarpone, salt, and lemon zest. Spread mascarpone mixture evenly on bottom of cooled crust.

4 Arrange berries on top of mascarpone mixture.

Prep time: *15 minutes*
Hands-off cooking time: *10-20 minutes (for crust)*
Serves *8*

Nutrition Snapshot
Per serving: 354 calories, 17 g fat, 10 g saturated fat, 7 g protein, 44 g carbs, 6 g fiber, 16 g sugar, 391 mg sodium

Tip: *It's best to assemble this tart no more than 2 hours before serving so the crust doesn't get soggy. You can bake the crust and mix the filling ahead of time, leaving everything waiting in the fridge for quick assembly.*

Lemon Drop Martini

The Lemon Drop became popular in 1970s California and its combined lemony flavors and kick of vodka has since earned it a spot as a classic favorite drink. Both Simple Syrup and agave nectar dissolve easily in cold liquids, making this an easy drink to mix. If using sugar instead, use a shaker to dissolve.

2 oz vodka (4 Tbsp)

½ oz triple sec or limoncello (1 Tbsp)

1 oz fresh lemon juice (2 Tbsp), saving a wedge or the peel for garnish

2 tsp Simple Syrup or 1 tsp agave nectar

1-2 Tbsp sugar (optional, for the rim)

1   Place sugar in a shallow dish. Rub rim of a martini glass or short tumbler with lemon and dip into sugar.

2   Fill glass with ice cubes and add vodka, triple sec, lemon juice, and simple syrup, stirring gently to combine.

Prep time: *5 minutes*
Serves *1*

Nutrition Snapshot

Per serving: 211 calories, 0 g fat, 0 g saturated fat, 0 g protein, 14 g carbs, 0 g fiber, 6 g sugar, 0 mg sodium

Helpful Tip: *To make your own simple syrup, mix equal parts sugar and water. Heat mixture slowly over low heat, stirring until sugar dissolves. Cool to room temperature. 1 cup water + 1 cup sugar yields 1 ⅓ cups simple syrup. Store refrigerated in a covered bottle.*

No Moo Mousse

Vegans and lactose-intolerant folks everywhere – rejoice! This delicious chocolate mousse has rich, intense flavor from dark chocolate and creaminess from light coconut milk rather than heavy dairy products. In addition, the light coconut milk has a fraction of the calories of heavy cream, making this mousse a better choice for anyone counting calories.

Mousse
2 (3.5-oz) bars dark bittersweet chocolate, such as Valrhona 71% Cacao
1 (14-oz) can Light Coconut Milk
2 Tbsp Captain Morgan Original Spiced Rum (optional; do not use regular rum)

Topping
Any selection of fresh berries or mango

1 Melt chocolate in one of two ways:

   - **Microwave method:** Break up chocolate bars into squares (8 squares for each bar) and place in a small Pyrex bowl. Microwave for 1 minute and stir. Repeat with 30-second intervals, stirring after every interval until fully melted. Wait a minute between intervals to let the heat of the bowl dissipate. Melting 2 chocolate bars should take about a total of 2 minutes. Be careful not to burn the chocolate.

   - **Stovetop method:** Place 3-4 cups water in a pot and bring to a boil. Place a glass Pyrex bowl on top of boiling water (bottom of bowl should not touch water) and place chocolate pieces in bowl. Steam from boiling water will gently melt chocolate without scorching it.

2 Add coconut milk and rum to blender. Pour melted chocolate into blender and blend right away for about 30 seconds. Pour mousse into individual cups or ramekins and place in fridge for two hours. If leaving them in the fridge longer than a couple of hours or making it the day before, cover mousse cups with plastic wrap.

3 If desired, top each mousse cup generously with fresh fruit right before serving

Prep time: *10 minutes. Make at least 2 hours ahead of time*

Nutrition Snapshot
Per serving: 179 calories, 12 g fat, 8 g saturated fat, 2 g protein, 10 g carbs, 4 g fiber, 8 g sugar, 37 mg sodium

Good-for-you Strawberries and Cream

Silky, rich Greek yogurt replaces whipped cream in this variation of the classic strawberries and cream. Adding only a sprinkle of sugar to strawberries releases their juices, creating a sweet, syrupy concoction in just minutes. The longer you leave the strawberries, the juicier they will become.

1 cup strawberries, diced or sliced
1 tsp brown sugar
½ cup plain Greek yogurt
1 tsp honey
1 tsp lemon juice

1 Toss together strawberries and sugar. Set aside for 10 minutes.

2 Combine yogurt, honey, and lemon juice. Pour over strawberries. Drizzle extra honey if desired.

Prep time: *10 minutes,* **Serves** *1*

Nutrition Snapshot
Per serving: 217 calories, 10 g fat, 6 g saturated fat, 6 g protein, 29 g carbs, 3 g fiber, 21 g sugar, 58 mg sodium

Gluten Free

Mango Lassi

A mango lassi is basically a smoothie made with yogurt and mango. Flaxseed oil is optional if you want to add some healthy omega-3 essential fatty acids to your morning. Don't worry when you read the word "fatty" – omega-3's increase your body's metabolic rate, actually helping burn excess fats in your body! You'll find flaxseed oil in the supplements section at Trader Joe's, not with the oils.

1 cup frozen Mango Chunks
1 cup plain or vanilla yogurt (nonfat or regular)
¼ cup orange juice
1 tsp agave nectar or honey
1 Tbsp flaxseed oil (optional)

1 Add ingredients to a blender and blend until smooth.

Prep time: *5 minutes,* **Serves** *2*

Nutrition Snapshot
Per serving: 132 calories, 0 g fat, 0 g saturated fat, 6 g protein, 28 g carbs, 2 g fiber, 26 g sugar, 82 mg sodium

Frozen Tiramisu

If you love tiramisu but don't have the time to make it, here is a luscious frozen version that can be assembled in minutes and requires no pastry skills. Even better, it doesn't use raw eggs like the traditional version. Ice cream aficionados say they like our version better than the traditional one.

½ gallon vanilla ice cream or gelato
½ cup strong coffee (instant is fine: mix 1 Tbsp instant coffee into ½ cup hot water)
¼ cup white or dark rum
1 box Soft Lady Fingers (24 cookies)
1 oz bittersweet chocolate such as Valrhona 71% Cacao bar, coarsely grated
Cocoa powder or ground cinnamon (optional)

1   Soften ice cream in microwave for 1 minute, using the defrost setting. Or, let ice cream soften on your countertop for 20 minutes.

2   Meanwhile, mix coffee and rum in a shallow bowl. Working with 1-2 ladyfingers at a time, soak ladyfingers in coffee mixture for 2-3 seconds on each side and then place into freezer-safe pan, making an even layer. (An 8 x 8-inch square pan works well for this recipe. 12 ladyfingers, or two rows of 6 cookies, cover the bottom perfectly.)

3   Stir softened ice cream until smooth. Pour half the ice cream into pan and spread evenly.

4   Place another layer of soaked ladyfingers (2 rows of 6 cookies) on top of ice cream. Cover ladyfingers with remaining ice cream. Cover top layer with plastic wrap and freeze tiramisu for at least 4 hours.

5   When ready to serve, remove plastic wrap and discard. Garnish with grated chocolate, cocoa powder, and ground cinnamon.

Variation: *If you love the flavor of coffee, try using coffee ice cream instead of vanilla ice cream.*

Prep time: *15 minutes (not including thawing)*
Serves *8*

Nutrition Snapshot
Per serving: 367 calories, 17 g fat, 10 g saturated fat, 6 g protein, 45 g carbs, 1 g fiber, 38 g sugar, 133 mg sodium

Almond Pudding

You may never have had a pudding like this before, made only with almond meal and no rice or wheat. A touch of Italian and a touch of Turkish, this pudding is flavored with the great taste and texture of ground almonds and subtle hints of coffee, cinnamon, and vanilla. Some claim it's perfect for an indulgent breakfast! Top with whipped cream, Organic Apricot Orange Fruit Spread, or enjoy plain.

2 cups almond meal

4 cups whole milk

1 cup sugar

1 tsp cinnamon

1 tsp instant coffee

1 tsp pure vanilla extract

1   Mix all the ingredients in a medium saucepan over medium heat and stir until smooth.

2   As it just begins to simmer, turn heat to low and continue stirring occasionally for 20 minutes, making sure pudding is not sticking to sides or bottom.

3   Pour into 8 small bowls or cups and chill in the fridge for a couple of hours until set. If leaving overnight, cover with plastic wrap.

Cooking time: *25 minutes*
Serves *8*

Nutrition Snapshot

Per serving: 354 calories, 19 g fat, 3 g saturated fat, 11 g protein, 37 g carbs, 3 g fiber, 32 g sugar, 49 mg sodium

G
Gluten Free

Nearly Instant Homemade Mango Ice Cream

Yes, it's possible to make ice cream at home without an ice cream maker and in just minutes! The trick is to combine frozen fruit and half-and-half (or heavy cream) in a food processor. The result is a soft ice cream, made with any fruit flavor you like. Although the texture is not identical to commercial ice cream, the flavor is outstanding, and it just can't get simpler to make ice cream.

12 oz (about half the bag) Frozen Mango Chunks
²/₃ cup half-and-half
¼ cup sugar

1   Combine half-and-half and sugar and stir for 30 seconds until sugar starts to dissolve.

2   Do not thaw mango; for this recipe it should be frozen hard. Add frozen mango to a food processor, and process just to chop it up roughly. Add half-and-half and process until mixture is smooth (1-2 minutes).

3   Serve right away. Or, for a hard-frozen ice cream, pour into a freezer-safe container and place in freezer for about 2 hours. Stir it every 30 minutes until it freezes, helping to break up ice crystals that may form.

Variation: *Use frozen strawberries or any other frozen fruit instead of mango. Experiment with unusual fruits and combinations for unique ice creams all your own! For a richer ice cream, substitute heavy cream.*

Prep time: *5 minutes*
Makes *4 (½-cup) servings*

Nutrition Snapshot
Per serving: 157 calories, 5 g fat, 3 g saturated fat, 2 g protein, 27 g carbs, 1 g fiber, 21 g sugar, 17 mg sodium

Vanilla Chai Bread Pudding

If you recoil in fear when you see the words "ramekin" or "water bath" in a recipe, you're not alone. Many people assume those recipes are for veteran chefs, but in reality they are quite simple. Here is an easy yet unique bread pudding, flavored with Trader Joe's delicious chai mix and sweetened with a little agave nectar.

6 cups cubed challah bread (a little more than ½ of a 1-lb challah loaf)
3 eggs
1 cup heavy cream
1 ½ Tbsp Spicy Chai Latte Mix powder
1 tsp vanilla extract
¼ cup agave nectar
Candied ginger (optional, for garnish)
Six 6-oz ramekins (3.5-inch diameter)

1. Preheat oven to 350° F.
2. Place cubed bread in medium sized bowl.
3. In a separate bowl, combine eggs, cream, chai powder, vanilla, and agave. Whisk together until mixture is smooth and all chai powder has dissolved.
4. Pour chai mixture over bread and let soak for 10 minutes. Do not stir since that will create a mush. Once or twice, using a large spoon or spatula, gently flip some of the bread over so mixture soaks in evenly.
5. Fill each well-buttered or oiled ramekin with bread mixture. Press gently to compact slightly.
6. Place ramekins in baking dish. Create a water bath by filling baking dish with hot water. Water should reach halfway up sides of ramekins.
7. Place in oven (carefully!), drape with foil, and bake for about 30 minutes until bread pudding is firm in the center.
8. Pop out of ramekins if desired. Serve warm with ice cream, frozen yogurt, or drizzle with chocolate sauce. Garnish with pieces of candied ginger.

Prep time: *15 minutes*
Hands-off cooking time: *30 minutes*
Serves *6*

Nutrition Snapshot
Per serving: 347 calories, 19 g fat, 10 g saturated fat, 6 g protein, 36 g carbs, 1 g fiber, 16 g sugar, 227 mg sodium

Lemon Tart with Fresh Berries

Lemon curd is an English specialty spread, creamy and rich with the flavor of fresh lemons. Fresh fruit is a nice balance to the tang of lemon curd. For an easy tart, spread the lemon curd on a cooked pastry crust and top with fresh berries (and even ice cream or whipped cream). This tart will last just fine in the fridge and can be made ahead of time. Keep a jar of lemon curd in the pantry and a pie crust in the freezer, ready to go as a last-minute dessert. If the Queen drops by for high tea, you'll be prepared.

1 frozen pie crust
1 (10.5-oz) jar Lemon Curd
Fresh seasonal berries

1 Thaw crust and press into an 11-inch tart pan or shallow pie pan. Bake according to single-crust instructions on box.

2 Remove crust from oven and cool completely.

3 Spread lemon curd in an even layer across baked crust. Fill with berries. Chill for later, or serve right away.

Prep and cooking time: *15 minutes (not counting cooling time)*
Serves *6*

Nutrition Snapshot
Per serving: 409 calories, 21 g fat, 12 g saturated fat, 5 g protein, 50 g carbs, 1 g fiber, 32 g sugar, 305 mg sodium

Peachy Sangria

A white version of its classic cousin, Sangria, this peachy drink is light and crisp – great for brunch or a light dinner on the patio. Make it ahead of time to allow the fruity flavors to meld.

1 bottle dry white wine, such as Barefoot Pinot Grigio
½ cup Montbisou Pêches or other peach liqueur (optional)
2 Tbsp sugar
1-2 peaches, unpeeled and cut into wedges
1 cup assorted colors grapes, halved
1 cup mineral water or club soda

1 Combine wine, liqueur, sugar, and fruit in a glass pitcher. Place in fridge for at least 4 hours.

2 Just before serving, stir in mineral water.

Prep time: *10 minutes*
Serves *4*

Nutrition Snapshot
Per serving: 213 calories, 0 g fat, 0 g saturated fat, 1 g protein, 23 g carbs, 1 g fiber, 14 g sugar, 1 mg sodium

Gluten Free

Chocolate Coffee Fudge

This rich fudge is ridiculously easy. It calls for only three ingredients and takes just a few minutes to prepare. Wona sent this fudge to her husband's office for a chocolate-themed contest and it won, beating out a multitude of extravagant desserts. When she was asked for the recipe, she was almost embarrassed to share it given how simple it is! A hint of coffee enhances the taste of the chocolate and adds complexity to the fudge. (Try adding a small amount of instant coffee the next time you make any chocolate dessert.)

1 (14-oz) can sweetened condensed milk
2 Tbsp instant coffee
½ Tbsp water
1 (12-oz) bag semi-sweet chocolate chips

1   Heat condensed milk in a heavy saucepan over medium heat.

2   Dissolve instant coffee in water (it will be thick) and stir into condensed milk.

3   Add chocolate chips, reduce flame to low, and stir until melted and smooth. Be careful not to scorch fudge.

4   Pour into an oiled 8x8-inch pan. Chill in fridge until set, about 2 hours.

Prep time: *5-10 minutes,*
Makes *about 20 small pieces*

Nutrition Snapshot
Per piece: 154 calories, 6 g fat, 4 g saturated fat, 3 g protein, 23 g carbs, 1 g fiber, 20 g sugar, 20 mg sodium

G
Gluten Free

Tip: *When cutting fudge, a plastic knife is easiest. If using a regular knife, wipe it clean in between cuts. Then use a spatula to lift out pieces. You can also line pan with wax paper for easier removal.*

"A Hint of Coffee" Brownies with Café Latte Glaze

Adding a touch of coffee to chocolate desserts intensifies the chocolate flavor and takes it to a new level. We adapted our recipe from an espresso brownie recipe by Giada De Laurentiis. We use Trader Joe's rich brownie mix and add instant coffee. Finish it by drizzling on a café latte glaze.

1 (16-oz) pkg Brownie Truffle Baking Mix (plus 2 eggs and 1 stick butter to prepare mix)
2 Tbsp instant coffee

Café latte glaze
1 Tbsp instant coffee
1 Tbsp water
½ tsp vanilla
1 Tbsp butter at room temperature
⅔ cup powdered sugar

1 Prepare brownies according to instructions, but when mixing together butter and eggs, whisk in instant coffee. Bake and cool completely.

2 To prepare glaze, combine coffee, water, vanilla, and butter, whisking to combine. Slowly whisk in powdered sugar, little by little, until glaze is thick but still pourable. Drizzle over entire pan of brownies, or cut brownies into pieces and drizzle over each piece. Place in fridge until glaze sets.

Variation: *Use Trader Joe's Mini Milk Chocolate Peanut Butter Cups to create a gooey chocolate-peanut-butter version. After preparing the Brownie Truffle Baking Mix, stir in 1 cup peanut butter cups into the batter and bake as directed.*

Prep time: *15 minutes*
Hands-off cooking time: *25-30 minutes*
Serves *16*

Nutrition Snapshot
Per serving: 222 calories, 9 g fat, 5 g saturated fat, 2 g protein, 22 g carbs, 1 g fiber, 27 g sugar, 59 mg sodium

Substitute Trader Joe's Gluten-Free Brownie Mix

Mighty Mojito

The mojito is a classic Cuban drink that balances strong rum with sweetness, fresh lime juice, and cool mint leaves. This refreshing drink is served over crushed ice and typically enjoyed in warmer weather. Don't chop the mint leaves or they will muddy the drink with mint specks. Instead, bruise them to release the intoxicating aroma and oils.

8-10 mint leaves

2 Tbsp fresh lime juice

2 oz rum (¼ cup)

1 tsp honey or agave nectar

²/₃ cup French Market Limeade or other lime soda

1 cup crushed ice

1   Place mint leaves in a glass, tearing large leaves in two. Add lime juice. Use a muddler or wooden spoon to crush mint leaves against glass and release juices.

2   Add rum and honey. Stir well.

3   Add lime soda and crushed ice. Stir again and garnish with additional mint leaves and lime slices if desired.

Prep time: *5 minutes*
Serves *1*

Nutrition Snapshot

Per serving: 228 calories, 0 g fat, 0 g saturated fat, 1 g protein, 26 g carbs, 1 g fiber, 23 g sugar, 26 mg sodium

G
Gluten Free

Super-Food Fruit Smoothie **236**

Goat Cheese Scramble **238**

Quick and Creamy Quinoa Cereal **241**

Yogurt Parfait **243**

Swiss Muesli **244**

Veggie Masala Scramble **247**

Baked French Toast Casserole **248**

Mushroom Basil Frittata **251**

Purple Porridge **252**

Orange Cranberry Scones **255**

Breakfast

Super-Food Fruit Smoothie

We love a good smoothie as a healthful and easy way to start the day. For the most part, we tend to make them with ingredients on hand, but we've found a few favorites we repeat again and again. Kids love smoothies too, and it's an easy way to experiment with healthy additions. This particular smoothie is primarily made of fruit and yogurt but has a few additions that round it out. The protein in tofu and yogurt balances the fruit carbohydrates. Flax oil is a viable source of essential fatty acids, and Very Green powder packs a punch of vegetable minerals, vitamins, enzymes, and antioxidants.

1 ripe banana, peeled
1 cup plain yogurt
½ cup frozen blueberries
1 cup frozen Mango Chunks
⅓ cup soft/regular tofu (about a ¾-inch slice off the end)
1 Tbsp Very Green powdered supplement
2 Tbsp flax oil
1 Tbsp honey
½ cup almond milk or milk of your choice

1 Add all ingredients to a blender. Blend for a couple of minutes or until smooth.

2 For a delicious smoothie bowl with a little added crunch, pour in a bowl and top with a few Tbsp of granola, such as Granola & the Three Berries, and some fresh berries.

Prep time: *10 minutes*
Serves *4*

Nutrition Snapshot
Per serving: 219 calories, 9 g fat, 1 g saturated fat, 8 g protein, 29 g carbs, 2 g fiber, 21 g sugar, 59 mg sodium

G
Gluten Free

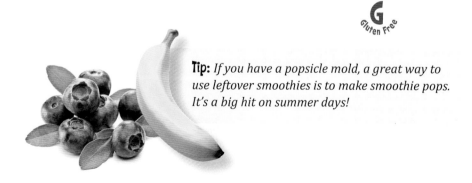

Tip: *If you have a popsicle mold, a great way to use leftover smoothies is to make smoothie pops. It's a big hit on summer days!*

Goat Cheese Scramble

When you're looking for that extra something to perk up scrambled eggs, try adding creamy goat cheese and herbs. The light tang of goat cheese adds a luxurious touch. It's an easy and impressive dish to add to your brunch spread.

12 eggs
¼ cup milk or water
½ tsp salt
¼ tsp black pepper
1 Tbsp vegetable oil or butter
4 oz goat cheese, crumbled
2 Tbsp chopped fresh chives, basil, or oregano

1   In a large bowl, beat eggs with milk, salt, and pepper.

2   Heat oil in a large skillet over medium heat. Add egg mixture to skillet and turn heat to low. Using a spatula, scrape bottom of pan frequently to keep eggs moving as they cook. The trick to delicious scrambled eggs is to cook them slowly, over low heat.

3   When eggs are almost done (but still runny), sprinkle with goat cheese and stir to let the heat melt the cheese. Sprinkle with fresh herbs.

Prep time: *15 minutes*
Serves *6*

Nutrition Snapshot
Per serving: 219 calories, 9 g fat, 1 g saturated fat, 8 g protein, 29 g carbs, 2 g fiber, 21 g sugar, 59 mg sodium

G
Gluten Free

Quick and Creamy Quinoa Cereal

Quinoa (pronounced KEEN-wah) is a nice alternative to oatmeal in the morning; just a little bit is very satisfying. High in protein and gluten free, quinoa is healthy and has a nice seedy texture and nutty taste. Start with our recipe below and then experiment with your own additions.

1 cup uncooked quinoa, rinsed and drained

2 cups water

½ tsp cinnamon

½ tsp vanilla extract or flavoring

1 ripe banana, peeled and diced

½ cup dried Golden Berry Blend or Dried Berry Medley

¼ cup slivered almonds

1   Add quinoa, water, banana, cinnamon, and vanilla to a small saucepan. Bring to a simmer and cook for 15 minutes or until all the water is absorbed.

2   Mix in nuts and dried berries. Top with cream, milk, honey, Turbinado sugar, or maple syrup as desired.

Prep time: *5 minutes*
Hands-off cooking time: *15 minutes*
Serves *4*

Nutrition Snapshot
Per serving: 315 calories, 7 g fat, 0 g saturated fat, 8 g protein, 58 g carbs, 6 g fiber, 21 g sugar, 5 mg sodium

Yogurt Parfait

We really like the crunch and dense goodness of granola in this combination with yogurt and fresh berries, but nearly any cereal will do. If you don't have fresh berries on hand, use your favorite berry jam.

½ cup cup plain yogurt, such as Plain Cream Line Yogurt, or Greek Style Honey Yogurt

¾ cup granola (we like Granola & the 3 Berries or Pecan Praline Granola)

¾ cup fresh berries in season

1　Layer yogurt, granola, and berries in a clear glass, alternating layers a few times.

Prep time: *5 minutes*
Serves *1*

Nutrition Snapshot

Per serving: 333 calories, 11 g fat, 4 g saturated fat, 9 g protein, 51 g carbs, 6 g fiber, 24 g sugar, 95 mg sodium

Use gluten-free granola, available in several varieties

Swiss Muesli

Muesli was first introduced in 1900 by a Swiss physician who served it in his hospital as part of a healthy diet for his patients. Believe us, this tastes nothing like hospital food! Fresh oats combined with crisp apples and nuts are soaked overnight for a truly satisfying breakfast. Full of whole grains, calcium, vitamins, and fiber, this is a power-packed breakfast that gets your day started right. What a bonus that it tastes great too.

2 cups rolled oats

2 cups skim, lowfat, or whole milk, soy milk, or almond milk

½ cup orange juice (optional)

1 cup lowfat or whole plain yogurt

2 Tbsp honey

1 crisp apple, chopped in small pieces (keep the peel on for extra fiber)

⅓ cup sliced almonds

1 Whisk milk, orange juice, yogurt, and honey in a glass bowl.

2 Stir in oats, apples, almonds, and raisins.

3 Soak overnight in refrigerator to allow oats to soften. Muesli will be thick after soaking, and can be thinned with additional milk before serving.

Prep time: *10 minutes*
Serves *8*

Nutrition Snapshot

Per serving: 80 calories, 2 g fat, 0 g saturated fat, 3 g protein, 13 g carbs, 1 g fiber, 5 g sugar, 25 mg sodium

G Gluten Free

Use gluten-free oats

Veggie Masala Scramble

Trader Joe's Vegetable Masala Burgers make a great combination with eggs. The burgers are flavorful and only very slightly spice, becoming even milder when scrambled with eggs. Start the morning off with a tasty scramble—you can even wrap it in a tortilla, breakfast burrito style, for breakfast on the go.

1 frozen Vegetable Masala Burger
2 large eggs
5-6 crimini or white mushrooms (optional)

1   Heat the veggie burger per package instructions (An easy way is to heat in a non-stick skillet with just a touch of spray oil.)

2   While the burger is heating, slice the mushrooms and beat the eggs.

3   When the burger is done, remove, chop up, and set aside.

4   Saute the mushrooms in the pan. When softened, add the eggs and cook over low heat until eggs start to set up. Stir in the chopped burger and remove from heat. Let residual heat of pan finish cooking the eggs.

Prep and cooking time: *10 minutes*
Serves *1*

Nutrition Snapshot
Per serving: 80 calories, 2 g fat, 0 g saturated fat, 3 g protein, 13 g carbs, 1 g fiber, 5 g sugar, 25 mg sodium

G
Gluten Free

Baked French Toast Casserole

For those weekend mornings when you have time for a more leisurely breakfast, try this twist on traditional French toast. This dish is easy enough for a casual family breakfast and elegant enough for an upscale brunch. It's quick to assemble, and you don't have to stand over the stove cooking each piece individually.

1 (1-lb) challah loaf or brioche loaf
2 cups whole milk
4 eggs
1 tsp cinnamon
2 tsp vanilla extract
¼ cup brown sugar
1 Tbsp Turbinado sugar for sprinkling on top

1 Preheat oven to 350° F.

2 Oil or butter a 9x13-inch glass baking dish (use an 8x8-inch dish if using a smaller loaf).

3 Tear loaf into bite-size pieces and place in pan.

4 Whisk together milk, eggs, cinnamon, vanilla, and brown sugar. Pour mixture over bread.

5 Wait a few minutes to let the liquid soak into the bread, gently tossing bread around a little to soak evenly. Sprinkle top with sugar.

6 Bake in oven for 35-40 minutes, uncovered. It will puff up when done.

Prep time: *10 minutes,*
Hands-off cooking time: *35-40 minutes*
Serves *8*

Nutrition Snapshot
Per serving: 279 calories, 9 g fat, 2 g saturated fat, 9 g protein, 41 g carbs, 2 g fiber, 13 g sugar, 321 mg sodium

Mushroom Basil Frittata

A frittata is similar to a quiche, but without the crust. You can use virtually any ingredients you have on hand—it's a great way to use leftover veggies. This version uses criminis, which are actually baby Portabella mushrooms. They have more flavor and nutrients than standard mushrooms, but for a milder flavor, you can use white button mushrooms or another variety of your choice. This versatile dish can be served around the clock. It's great for breakfast with a warm mug of coffee, or for dinner with a green salad.

3 cups fresh Sliced Crimini Mushrooms

3 Tbsp butter

8 eggs

⅓ cup whole milk or heavy cream

½ tsp salt

¼ tsp black pepper

½ cup fresh basil leaves, roughly chopped

½ cup Quattro Formaggio shredded cheese

1   Preheat oven to 350° F.

2   Melt butter in a 10-inch nonstick oven-safe skillet over medium heat. Add mushrooms and cook for 5 minutes.

3   While mushrooms are cooking, whisk eggs, milk, salt, and pepper until combined. Mix in basil and cheese.

4   Pour egg mixture into hot skillet, over the cooked mushrooms. Place in oven for 30 minutes or until egg is set. Eggs will puff up while cooking but will deflate when you take it out of the oven.

Prep time: *10 minutes*
Hands-off cooking time: *30 minutes*
Serves *6*

Nutrition Snapshot
Per serving: 235 calories, 20 g fat, 10 g saturated fat, 12 g protein, 3 g carbs, 0 g fiber, 1 g sugar, 368 mg sodium

Gluten Free

Purple Porridge

With a touch of vanilla and cinnamon, this oatmeal is naturally sweetened with banana. Sweet blueberries turn the porridge purple, appealing to kids (or the kid in all of us). Fresh blueberries can be substituted, but the intense color is most easily released by frozen blueberries. As an added bonus, extra frozen blueberries can be stirred in right before eating as a way to cool a steaming bowl of porridge quickly! Banana provides plenty of natural sweetness, but a little bit of maple syrup, agave nectar, honey, or sweetened almond milk can be added for an even sweeter taste.

½ cup Quick Cook Steel Cut Oats
1 ½ cup water
1 ripe banana, chopped
1 tsp vanilla
Sprinkle of cinnamon
½ cup frozen blueberries

1   Add all ingredients to a small saucepan. Bring to a boil and reduce to a simmer. Cook for 5-7 minutes, or until water is absorbed.

2   Serve with milk, drizzling maple syrup, agave nectar, or honey on top as desired.

Prep and cooking time: *10 minutes*
Serves *2*

Nutrition Snapshot
Per serving: 235 calories, 3 g fat, 1 g saturated fat, 6 g protein, 46 g carbs, 6 g fiber, 12 g sugar, 1 mg sodium

G
Gluten Free

*Use gluten-free
steel cut oats*

Orange Cranberry Scones

Perfect for brunch or afternoon tea, these easy scones are light and flaky. Serve with Trader Joe's Lemon Curd or any fruit jam for extra flavor. Of course, they're also delicious simply on their own.

3 ½ cups Buttermilk Pancake Mix
3 Tbsp sugar
Zest of 1 orange or 1 Tbsp orange marmalade (optional)
¼ cup unsalted butter, chilled and diced into small squares
¾ cup whole milk
¾ cup dried Orange Flavored Cranberries

1   Preheat oven to 400° F.

2   Mix pancake mix, sugar, and orange zest or marmalade. Add butter and cut into the flour mixture, using a fork or pastry knife, until the butter is the size of peas. (If you have a food processor, it will do this job in just seconds, but it's not necessary.)

3   Add milk and combine. Fold in cranberries. Dough will be quite sticky.

4   Place dough on a well-floured surface. Pat dough into a 4 x 16-inch rectangle; dough will be approximately ¾ inch thick. Cut rectangle into four 4 x 4-inch squares. Cut each square diagonally.

5   Place scones on a cookie sheet and bake for 12 minutes or until golden brown.

Prep time: *15 minutes*
Hands-off cooking time: *12 minutes*
Makes *8 scones*

Nutrition Snapshot
Per scone: 310 calories, 9 g fat, 4 g saturated fat, 5 g protein, 51 g carbs, 1 g fiber, 19 g sugar, 800 mg sodium

Recipe Index

A

"A Hint of Coffee" Brownies with Café Latte Glaze, 230
Addictive Tacos, 148
Almond
    Bread, 187
    Pudding, 221
All Mixed Up Margaritas, 198
Alla Checca, Pasta, 81
Anytime Mediterranean Pasta, 101
Apple Tart, Simple, 207
Apricot Baked Brie, 13
Artichoke Dip, Kickin', 35
Arugula
    Pesto Pasta, 159
    Salad with Pine Nuts and Parmesan, 69
Asian Dumpling Soup, 52
Asparagus with Tomatoes and Feta, Roasted, 165
Avocado Salad, Endive, Beet, and, 41

B

Bake(d)
    Eggplant Zucchini, 167
    French Toast Casserole, 248
    Sweet Potato Fries, 174
    Tamale, 125
Balsamic Roasted Fennel, 170
Basil
    Cake, Lemon, 193
    Frittata, Mushroom, 251
    Wrap, Mozzarella, 156
Bean
    and Veggie Casserole, Corny-Copia, 92
    Burger, Black, 82
    Cornbread, Black, 166
    Salsa (Caviar, California), 26
    Soup, Black, 48
    White Lightning Chili, 147
Beet
    and Avocado Salad, Endive, 41
    and Mozzarella Salad (Winter Caprese), 75
    It Mandarin Orange Salad, Can't, 66
Berries
    Berry Mascarpone Tart, Very, 210
    Good-for-you Strawberries and Cream, 216
    Lemon Tart with Fresh Berries, 226
    Purple Porridge, 252

Black Bean
    and Ricotta-Stuffed Portabellas, 135
    Burger, 82
    Cornbread, 166
    Soup, 48
Blue Cheese Dressing, Homemade, 72
Blueberry Cobbler, One Bowl Peach and, 204
Border Pizza, South of the, 136
Boursin Roasted Red Pepper Penne, 97
Bowl, Sushi, 126
Bread
    Almond, 187
    Monkey, 194
    Olive-Stuffed, 23
Bread Pudding,
    Honey, I Ate the Chocolate, 191
    Vanilla Chai, 225
Brie, Apricot Baked, 13
Broccoli Slaw, Crunchy, 169
Brownies with Café Latte Glaze, "A Hint of Coffee", 230
Brussels Sprouts, Pan-Toasted, 181
Bunless Burger, Portabella, 86
Burger
    Black Bean, 82
    Portabella Bunless, 86
    Veggie Masala Scramble, 247
Burrito, Southwest, 113

C

Cake
    Lemon Basil, 193
    Chocolate Lava, 200
California Caviar (Bean Salsa), 26
Calzone, Spinach Ricotta, 153
Can't Beet It Mandarin Orange Salad, 66
Caprese, Winter (Beet and Mozzarella Salad), 75
Casserole
    Baked French Toast, 248
    Corny-Copia Bean and Veggie, 92
    Tamale Bake, 125
Cauliflower with Olives, Roasted, 177
Caviar, California (Bean Salsa), 26
Cereal
    Quick and Creamy Quinoa, 241
    Swiss Muesli, 244
Chai Bread Pudding, Vanilla, 225
Checca, Pasta alla, 81

Cheese
    and Chutney Mini-Rolls, 25
    Apricot Baked Brie, 13
    Dressing, Homemade Blue, 72
    Goat Cheese Scramble, 238
    Mozzarella Basil Wrap, 156
    Tomato and Mozzarella Skewers, 19
    Roasted Red Pepper and Mozzarella Sandwich, 102
    Warm Goat Cheese Salad, 56
    Warm Honeyed Figs with Goat Cheese, 31
Cherries, Pine Nuts, and Spinach Salad, Life is a Bowl of, 59
Chia Energy Drink (Chia Fresca), 203
Chili
    Soy Chorizo, 110
    White Lightning, 147
Chocolate
    "A Hint of Coffee" Brownies with Café Latte Glaze, 230
    Bread Pudding, Honey I Ate the, 191
    Coffee Fudge, 229
    Lava Cake, 200
    No Moo Mousse, 214
    Truffle Pie with Joe-Joe's Crust, 197
Chorizo
    Chili, Soy, 110
    Tamale Bake, 125
Chutney Mini-Rolls, Cheese and, 25
Cobbler, One Bowl Peach & Blueberry, 204
Coconut
    Curried Vegetables, 171
    Rice, Loco for, 178
Coffee
    Brownies with Café Latte Glaze, A Hint of, 230
    Fudge, Chocolate, 229
    Shake, Low-Fat Wide Awake, 192
Cornbread, Black Bean, 166
Corny-Copia Bean and Veggie Casserole, 92
Couscous with Sun Dried Tomatoes, 182
Cranberry Scones, Orange, 255
Cream, Good-for-you Strawberries and, 216
Creamsicle Smoothie, Orange, 208
Creamy
    Lemony Linguine, 109
    Stuffed Mushroom Caps, 32
Crunchy Broccoli Slaw, 169
Curried Vegetables, Coconut, 171
Curry
    Hurry for, 85
    Vegetable Tikka Masala, 98

D

Dip
    Just Peachy, 24
    Kickin' Artichoke, 35
    Ten-Layer Mexican, 28

Dressing
    Citrus, 41
    Citrus Vinaigrette, 51
    Homemade Balsamic, 59
    Homemade Blue Cheese, 72
    Homemade Orange Champagne Vinaigrette, 66
    Lemon Vinaigrette, 55
Dumpling
    Gyoza Salad, 138
    Soup, Asian, 52

E

Easy Tofu Stir Fry, 104
Egg(s)
    Goat Cheese Scramble, 238
    Mushroom Basil Frittata, 251
    My Big Fat Greek Quiche, 155
    Salad Olovieh (Persian Egg Salad), 64
    Simply Quiche, 118
    Veggie Masala Scramble, 247
Eggplant
    Parmesan, 122
    Pisto Manchego, 20
    Zucchini Bake, 167
Endive, Beet, and Avocado Salad, 41
Energy Drink, Chia (Chia Fresca), 203

F

Fennel, Balsamic Roasted, 170
Figs with Goat Cheese, Warm Honeyed, 31
Five-Minute Shiitake Fried Rice, 142
French
    Lentil Soup, Le, 63
    Toast Casserole, Baked, 248
Fresca, Chia (Chia Energy Drink), 203
Fried Rice, Five-Minute Shiitake, 142
Fries, Baked Sweet Potato, 174
Frittata, Mushroom Basil, 251
Frozen Tiramisu, 218
Fudge, Chocolate Coffee, 229

G

Garlic, Roasted (Friends Be Damned), 14
Gazpacho, Notcho Ordinary, 68
Gnocchi with Spinach, Gnutmeg, 141
Gnutmeg Gnocchi with Spinach, 141
Goat Cheese
    Salad, Warm, 56
    Scramble, 238
    Warm Honeyed Figs with, 31
Good-for-you Strawberries and Cream, 216
Grapes, Green Waldorf Salad, 60
Greek Quiche, My Big Fat, 155
Green Waldorf Salad, 60
Grilled
    Lentil Wraps, 150
    Veggie Sandwich with Lemon Garlic Sauce, 89

Gyoza
    Asian Dumpling Soup, 52
    Salad, 138

H

Harvest Grains Vegetable Soup, 70
Hearts and Snaps Salad, 46
Homemade
    Blue Cheese Dressing, 72
    Hummus, 16
    Mango Ice Cream, Nearly Instant, 222
Honey
    I Ate the Chocolate Bread Pudding, 191
    Figs with Goat Cheese, Warm, 31
Hummus
    and Lentil Wrap, 145
    Homemade, 16
Hurry for Curry, 85

I

Ice Cream
    Frozen Tiramisu, 218
    Nearly Instant Homemade Mango, 222
Indian Spinach Pizza, 17
Italian Wedding Soup, 42

J

Joe-Joe-s Crust, Chocolate Truffle Pie with, 197
Just Peachy Dip, 24

K

Kickin' Artichoke Dip, 35

L

Lasagna, No-Prep Veggie, 128
Lassi, Mango, 217
Lava Cake, Chocolate, 200
Le French Lentil Soup, 63
Lemon
    Basil Cake, 193
    Drop Martini, 213
    Garlic Sauce, Grilled Veggie Sandwich with, 89
    Linguine, Creamy, 109
    Tart with Fresh Berries, 226
Lentil
    Addictive Tacos, 148
    Salad, Mediterranean, 47
    Soup, Le French, 63
    Wrap, Hummus and, 145
    Wraps, Grilled Lentil, 150
Life is a Bowl of Cherries, Pine Nuts, and Spinach Salad, 59
Lightning Chili, White, 147
Lime, Mighty Mojito, 233
Linguine, Creamy Lemony, 109
Loco for Coconut Rice, 178
Low-Fat Wide Awake Coffee Shake, 192

M

Mâche Salad, Posh, 55
Manchego, Pisto, 20
Mandarin Orange Salad, Can't Beet It, 66
Mango
    Ice Cream, Nearly Instant Homemade, 222
    Lassi, 217
    Salsa, Strawberry, 36
Margaritas, All Mixed Up, 198
Martini, Lemon Drop, 213
Masala
    Scramble, Veggie, 247
    Vegetable Tikka, 98
Mascarpone Tart, Very Berry, 210
Mediterranean
    Lentil Salad, 47
    Pasta, Anytime, 101
Mexican Dip, Ten-Layer, 28
Mighty Mojito, 233
Mini-Roll, Cheese & Chutney, 25
Mojito, Mighty, 233
Monkey Bread, 194
Moussaka, Mushroom, 132
Mousse, No Moo, 214
Mozzarella
    Basil Wrap, 156
    Salad, Beet and (Winter Caprese), 75
    Sandwich, Roasted Red Pepper and, 102
    Skewers, Tomato and, 19
Muesli, Swiss, 244
Mushroom
    Basil Frittata, 251
    Black Bean and Ricotta-Stuffed Portabellas, 135
    Caps, Creamy Stuffed, 32
    Creamy Lemony Linguine, 109
    Five-Minute Shiitake Fried Rice, 142
    Moussaka, 132
    Portabella Bunless Burger, 86
    Portabella "Philly Cheesesteak", 94
    Risotto, Shiitake, 121
My Big Fat Greek Quiche, 155

N

Nearly Instant Homemade Mango Ice Cream, 222
No Moo Mousse, 214
No-Prep Veggie Lasagna, 128
Notcho Ordinary Gazpacho, 68
Noodles, Peanutty Sesame, 160
Nutty Wild Rice Salad, 51

O

Oats
    Purple Porridge, 252
    Swiss Muesli, 244
Olive-Stuffed Bread, 23
Olovieh, Egg Salad (Persian Egg Salad), 64
One Bowl Peach & Blueberry Cobbler, 204

Orange
    Cranberry Scones, 255
    Creamsicle Smoothie, 208
    Salad, Can't Beet It Mandarin, 66
Oven Roasted Vegetables with Rosemary, 172

P

Pan-Toasted Brussels Sprouts, 181
Parfait, Yogurt, 243
Parmesan, Eggplant, 122
Pasta
    alla Checca, 81
    Anytime Mediterranean, 101
    Arugula Pesto, 159
    Boursin Roasted Red Pepper Penne, 97
    Gnutmeg Gnocchi with Spinach, 141
    No-Prep Veggie Lasagna, 128
    Salad, Spinach Pesto, 131
    with Sun Dried Tomatoes, Stir-Fried, 106
Peach(y)
    and Blueberry Cobbler, One Bowl, 204
    Dip, Just, 24
    Sangria, 227
Peanutty Sesame Noodles, 160
Penne, Boursin Roasted Red Pepper, 97
Pepper(s)
    Penne, Boursin Roasted Red, 97
    Pisto Manchego, 20
    Stuffed Red, 78
Pesto
    Pasta, Arugula, 159
    Pasta Salad, Spinach, 131
    Pita Pizza, 114
Philly Cheesesteak, Portabella, 94
Pie
    Lemon Tart with Fresh Berries, 226
    Simple Apple Tart, 207
    Very Berry Mascarpone Tart, 210
    with Joe-Joe's Crust, Chocolate Truffle, 197
Pine Nuts
    and Parmesan, Arugula Salad with, 69
    and Spinach Salad, Life is a Bowl of Cherries, 59
Pisto Manchego, 20
Pita Pizza, Pesto, 114
Pizza
    Indian Spinach, 17
    Pesto Pita, 114
    South of the Border, 136
    Thai, 90
Porridge, Purple, 252
Portabella /Portobello
    Black Bean and Ricotta-Stuffed, 135
    Bunless Burger, 86
    Creamy Stuffed Mushroom Caps, 32
    Philly Cheesesteak, 94
Posh Mâche Salad, 55
Potato Fries, Baked Sweet, 174

Potstickers
    Asian Dumpling Soup, 52
    Gyoza Salad, 138
Pudding
    Almond, 221
    Honey, I Ate the Chocolate Bread, 191
    Vanilla Chai Bread, 225
Purple Porridge, 252

Q

Quiche
    My Big Fat Greek, 155
    Simply, 118
Quick and Creamy Quinoa Cereal, 241
Quinoa Cereal, Quick and Creamy, 241

R

Red Pepper(s)
    and Mozzarella Sandwich, Roasted, 102
    Penne, Boursin Roasted, 97
    Stuffed, 78
Rice
    Five-Minute Shiitake Fried, 142
    Loco for Coconut, 178
    Salad, Nutty Wild, 51
    Shiitake Mushroom Risotto, 121
    Sushi Bowl, 126
Ricotta
    Calzone, Spinach, 153
    Stuffed Portabellas, Black Bean and, 135
Roasted
    Asparagus with Tomatoes and Feta, 165
    Cauliflower with Olives, 177
    Fennel, Balsamic, 170
    Garlic (Friends Be Damned), 14
    Red Pepper and Mozzarella Sandwich, 102
    Red Pepper Penne, Boursin, 97
    Vegetables with Rosemary, Oven, 172

S

Salad
    Arugula with Pine Nuts and Parmesan, 69
    Beet and Mozzarella (Winter Caprese), 75
    Can't Beet It Mandarin Orange, 66
    Crunchy Broccoli Slaw, 169
    Egg (Olovieh, Persian), 64
    Endive, Beet, and Avocado, 41
    Green Waldorf, 60
    Gyoza, 138
    Hearts and Snaps, 46
    Life is a Bowl of Cherries, Pine Nuts, and
        Spinach Salad, 59
    Mediterranean Lentil, 47
    Nutty Wild Rice, 51
    Olovieh (Persian Egg Salad), 64

Salad (cont.)
    Posh Mâche, 55
    Spinach Pesto Pasta, 131
    Warm Goat Cheese, 56
    Wasabi Tofu, 44
    Winter Caprese (Beet and Mozzarella), 75
Salsa
    Bean (Caviar, California), 26
    Strawberry Mango, 36

Sandwich
    Portabella "Philly Cheesesteak", 94
    Roasted Red Pepper and Mozzarella, 102
    with Lemon Garlic Sauce, Grilled Veggie, 89
Sangria, Peachy, 227
Scones, Orange Cranberry, 255
Scramble
    Goat Cheese, 238
    Veggie Masala, 247
Sesame
    Noodles, Peanutty, 160
    Toasted Sugar Snap Peas, 185
Shake, Low-Fat Wide Awake Coffee, 192
Shiitake
    Fried Rice, Five-Minute, 142
    Mushroom Risotto, 121
Simple Apple Tart, 207
Simply Quiche, 118
Skewers, Tomato and Mozzarella, 19
Slaw, Crunchy Broccoli, 169
Smoothie
    Mango Lassi, 217
    Orange Creamsicle, 208
    Super-Food Fruit, 236
Snaps Salad, Hearts and, 46
Soup
    Asian Dumpling, 52
    Black Bean, 48
    Harvest Grains Vegetable, 70
    Italian Wedding, 42
    Le French Lentil, 63
    Notcho Ordinary Gazpacho, 68
South of the Border Pizza, 136
Southwest Burrito, 113
Soy Chorizo
    Chili, 110
    Tamale Bake, 125
Spicy Szechuan Tofu, 117
Spinach
    Gnutmeg Gnocchi with, 141
    Pesto Pasta Salad, 131
    Pizza, Indian, 17
    Ricotta Calzone, 153
    Salad, Life is a Bowl of Cherries, Pine Nuts, and, 59
Stir Fry
    Easy Tofu, 104
    Pasta with Sun Dried Tomatoes, 106

Strawberry/Strawberries
    and Cream, Good-for-you, 216
    Mango Salsa, 36
Stuffed
    Bread, Olive-, 23
    Mushroom Caps, Creamy, 32
    Portabellas, Black Bean and Ricotta, 135
    Red Peppers, 78
Sugar Snap Peas, Sesame Toasted, 185
Sun Dried Tomatoes
    Couscous with, 182
    Spinach Ricotta Calzone, 153
    Stir-Fried Pasta with, 106
Super-Food Fruit Smoothie, 236
Sushi Bowl, 126
Sweet Potato Fries, Baked, 174
Swiss Muesli, 244
Szechuan Tofu, Spicy, 117

T

Tacos, Addictive, 148
Tamale Bake, 125
Tart
    Lemon with Fresh Berries, 226
    Simple Apple, 207
    Very Berry Mascarpone, 210
Ten-Layer Mexican Dip, 28
Thai Pizza, 90
Tikka Masala, Vegetable, 98
Tiramisu, Frozen, 218
Toasted
    Brussels Sprouts, Pan, 181
    Sugar Snap Peas, Sesame, 185
Tofu
    Salad, Wasabi, 44
    Spicy Szechuan, 117
    Stir Fry, Easy, 104
Tomato and Mozzarella Skewers, 19
Truffle Pie with Joe-Joe's Crust, Chocolate, 197

V

Vanilla Chai Bread Pudding, 225
Vegetable(s)
    Coconut Curried, 171
    Oven Roasted with Rosemary, 172
    Soup, Harvest Grains, 70
    Tikka Masala, 98
Veggie
    Casserole, Corny-Copia Bean and, 92
    Lasagna, No-Prep, 128
    Masala Scramble, 247
    Sandwich with Lemon Garlic Sauce, Grilled, 89
Very Berry Mascarpone Tart, 210

W

Waldorf Salad, Green, 60
Warm
    Goat Cheese Salad, 56
    Honeyed Figs with Goat Cheese, 31
Wasabi Tofu Salad, 44
Wedding Soup, Italian, 42
White Lightning Chili, 147
Wild Rice Salad, Nutty, 51
Winter Caprese (Beet and Mozzarella Salad), 75
Wrap(s)
    Grilled Lentil, 150
    Hummus and Lentil, 145
    Mozzarella Basil, 156

Y

Yogurt
    Good-for-you Strawberries and Cream, 216
    Mango Lassi, 217
    Parfait, 243
    Super-Food Fruit Smoothie, 236

Z

Zucchini Bake, Eggplant, 167

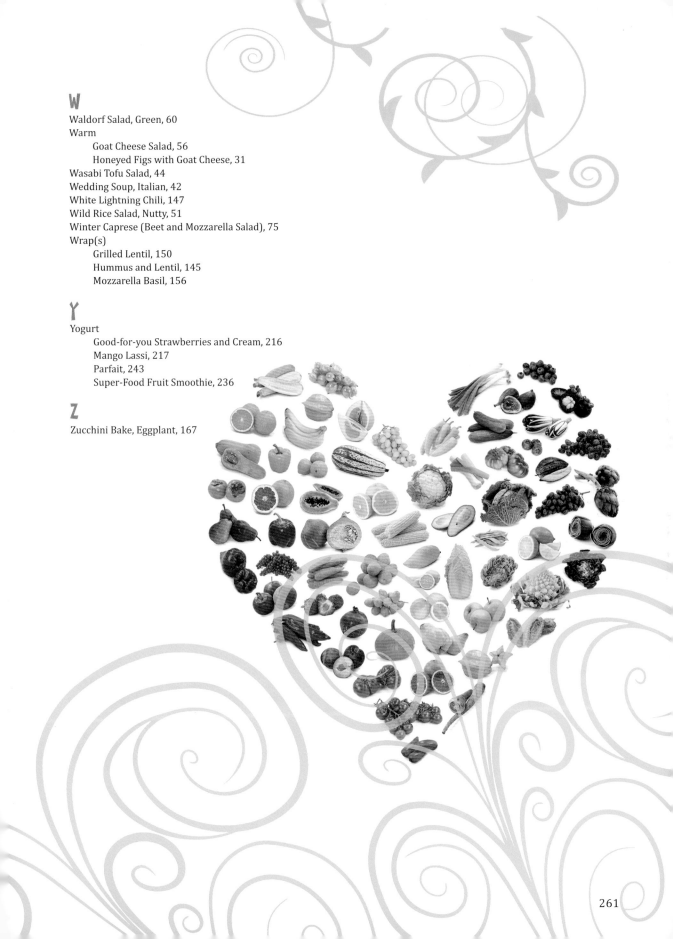

Gluten-Free Recipe Index

Recipes that are Gluten-Free or can easily be made
Gluten-Free (*) using simple substitutions

Appetizers

* Apricot Baked Brie, 13
California Caviar (Bean Salsa), 26
* Cheese & Chutney Mini-Rolls, 25
* Creamy Stuffed Mushroom Caps, 32
Homemade Hummus, 16
Just Peachy Dip, 24
Kickin' Artichoke Dip, 35
Pisto Manchego, 20
Roasted Garlic (Friends Be Damned), 14
Strawberry Mango Salsa, 36
Ten-Layer Mexican Dip, 28
Tomato and Mozzarella Skewers, 19
Warm Honeyed Figs with Goat Cheese, 31

Soups & Salads

Arugula Salad with Pine Nuts and Parmesan, 69
Black Bean Soup, 48
Can't Beet It Mandarin Orange Salad, 66
Egg Salad Olovieh (Persian Egg Salad), 64
Endive, Beat, and Avocado Salad, 41
Green Waldorf Salad, 60
Hearts and Snaps Salad, 46
Homemade Blue Cheese Dressing, 72
Le French Lentil Soup, 63
Life is a Bowl of Cherries, Pine Nuts, and Spinach, 59
Mediterranean Lentil Salad, 47
Nutty Wild Rice Salad, 51
Posh Mâche Salad, 55
Warm Goat Cheese Salad, 56
* Wasabi Tofu Salad, 44
Winter Caprese (Beet and Mozzarella Salad), 75

Main Meals

* Anytime Mediterranean Pasta, 101
* Arugula Pesto Pasta, 159
Black Bean and Ricotta-Stuffed Portabellas, 135
* Boursin Roasted Red Pepper Penne, 97
* Creamy Lemony Linguine, 109
* Five-Minute Shiitake Fried Rice, 142
* Grilled Veggie Sandwich with Lemon Garlic Sauce, 89
Hurry for Curry, 85
Mushroom Moussaka, 132
* My Big Fat Greek Quiche, 155
* Pasta alla Checca, 81
Portabella Bunless Burger, 86
* Roasted Red Pepper and Mozzarella Sandwich, 102

* Shiitake Mushroom Risotto, 121
* Soy Chorizo Chili, 110
* Spinach Pesto Pasta Salad, 131
* Stir-Fried Pasta with Sun Dried Tomatoes, 106
* Tamale Bake, 125
Vegetable Tikka Masala, 98
White Lightning Chili, 147

Sides

Almond Bread, 187
Baked Sweet Potato Fries, 174
Balsamic Roasted Fennel, 170
Coconut Curried Vegetables, 171
Crunchy Broccoli Slaw, 169
Loco for Coconut Rice, 178
Oven Roasted Vegetables with Rosemary, 172
* Pan-Toasted Brussels Sprouts, 181
Roasted Asparagus with Tomatoes and Feta, 165
Roasted Cauliflower with Olives, 177
Sesame Toasted Sugar Snap Pease, 185

Desserts & Drinks

* "A Hint of Coffee" Brownies with Café Latte Glaze, 230
All Mixed Up Margaritas, 198
Almond Pudding, 221
Chia Energy Drink (Chia Fresca), 203
Chocolate Coffee Fudge, 229
Good-for-you Strawberries and Cream, 216
Lemon Drop Martini, 213
Low-Fat Wide Awake Coffee Shake, 192
Mango Lassi, 217
Mighty Mojito, 233
Nearly Instant Homemade Mango Ice Cream, 222
No Moo Mousse, 214
Orange Creamsicle Smoothie, 208
Peachy Sangria, 227

Breakfast

Goat Cheese Scramble, 238
Mushroom Basil Frittata, 251
* Purple Porridge, 252
Quick and Creamy Quinoa Cereal, 241
Super-Food Fruit Smoothie, 236
* Swiss Muesli, 244
Veggie Masala Scramble, 247
* Yogurt Parfait, 243

Trader Joe's Store Locations

Arizona

Ahwatukee # 177
4025 E. Chandler Blvd., Ste. 38
Ahwatukee, AZ 85048
Phone: 480-759-2295

Glendale # 085
7720 West Bell Road
Glendale, AZ 85308
Phone: 623-776-7414

Mesa # 089
2050 East Baseline Rd.
Mesa, AZ 85204
Phone: 480-632-0951

Paradise Valley # 282
4726 E. Shea Blvd.
Phoenix, AZ 85028
Phone: 602-485-7788

**Phoenix
(Town & Country) # 090**
4821 N. 20th Street
Phoenix, AZ 85016
Phone: 602-912-9022

Prescott
252 Lee Blvd
Prescott, AZ 86303
Phone: 928-443-9075

Scottsdale (North) # 087
7555 E. Frank Lloyd Wright
N. Scottsdale, AZ 85260
Phone: 480-367-8920

Scottsdale # 094
6202 N. Scottsdale Road
Scottsdale, AZ 85253
Phone: 480-948-9886

Surprise # 092
14095 West Grand Ave.
Surprise, AZ 85374
Phone: 623-546-1640

Tempe # 093
6460 S. McClintock Drive
Tempe, AZ 85283
Phone: 480-838-4142

**Tucson
(Crossroads) # 088**
4766 East Grant Road
Tucson, AZ 85712
Phone: 520-323-4500

**Tucson (Wilmot &
Speedway)# 095**
1101 N. Wilmot Rd.
Suite #147
Tucson, AZ 85712
Phone: 520-733-1313

**Tucson (Campbell &
Limberlost) # 191**
4209 N. Campbell Ave.
Tucson, AZ 85719
Phone: 520-325-0069

Tucson - Oro Valley # 096
7912 N. Oracle
Oro Valley, AZ 85704
Phone: 520-797-4207

California

Agoura Hills
28941 Canwood Street
Agoura Hills, CA 91301
Phone: 818-865-8217

Alameda # 109
2217 South Shore Center
Alameda, CA 94501
Phone: 510-769-5450

Aliso Viejo # 195
The Commons
26541 Aliso Creek Road
Aliso Viejo, CA 92656
Phone: 949-643-5531

Arroyo Grande # 117
955 Rancho Parkway
Arroyo Grande, CA 93420
Phone: 805-474-6114

Bakersfield # 014
8200-C 21 Stockdale Hwy.
Bakersfield, CA 93311
Phone: 661-837-8863

Berkeley #186
1885 University Ave.
Berkeley, CA 94703
Phone: 510-204-9074

Bixby Knolls # 116
4121 Atlantic Ave.
Bixby Knolls, CA 90807
Phone: 562-988-0695

Brea # 011
2500 E. Imperial Hwy. Suite 177
Brea, CA 92821
Phone 714-257-1180

Brentwood # 201
5451 Lone Tree Way
Brentwood, CA 94513
Phone: 925-516-3044

Burbank # 124
214 East Alameda
Burbank, CA 91502
Phone: 818-848-4299

Camarillo # 114
363 Carmen Drive
Camarillo, CA 93010
Phone: 805-388-1925

Campbell # 073
1875 Bascom Avenue
Campbell, CA 95008
Phone: 408-369-7823

Capitola # 064
3555 Clares Street #D
Capitola, CA 95010
Phone: 831-464-0115

Carlsbad # 220
2629 Gateway Road
Carlsbad, CA 92009
Phone: 760-603-8473

Castro Valley # 084
22224 Redwood Road
Castro Valley, CA 94546
Phone: 510-538-2738

Cathedral City # 118
67-720 East Palm Cyn.
Cathedral City, CA 92234
Phone: 760-202-0090

Cerritos # 104
12861 Towne Center Drive
Cerritos, CA 90703
Phone: 562-402-5148

Chatsworth # 184
10330 Mason Ave.
Chatsworth, CA 91311
Phone: 818-341-3010

Chico # 199
801 East Ave., Suite #110
Chico, CA 95926
Phone: 530-343-9920

Chino Hills # 216
13911 Peyton Dr.
Chino Hills, CA 91709
Phone: 909-627-1404

Chula Vista # 120
878 Eastlake Parkway,
Suite 810
Chula Vista, CA 91914
Phone: 619-656-5370

Claremont # 214
475 W. Foothill Blvd.
Claremont, CA 91711
Phone: 909-625-8784

Clovis # 180
1077 N. Willow, Suite 101
Clovis, CA 93611
Phone: 559-325-3120

**Concord (Oak Grove
& Treat) # 083**
785 Oak Grove Road
Concord, CA 94518
Phone: 925-521-1134

Concord (Airport) # 060
1150 Concord Ave.
Concord, CA 94520
Phone: 925-689-2990

Corona # 213
2790 Cabot Drive, Ste. 165
Corona, CA 92883
Phone: 951-603-0299

Costa Mesa # 035
640 W. 17th Street
Costa Mesa, CA 92627
Phone: 949-642-5134

Culver City # 036
9290 Culver Blvd.
Culver City, CA 90232
Phone: 310-202-1108

Daly City # 074
417 Westlake Center
Daly City, CA 94015
Phone: 650-755-3825

Danville # 065
85 Railroad Ave.
Danville, CA 94526
Phone: 925-838-5757

Davis
885 Russell Blvd.
Davis, CA 95616
Phone: 530-757-2693

Eagle Rock # 055
1566 Colorado Blvd.
Eagle Rock, CA 90041
Phone: 323-257-6422

El Cerrito # 108
225 El Cerrito Plaza
El Cerrito, CA 94530
Phone: 510-524-7609

Elk Grove # 190
9670 Bruceville Road
Elk Grove, CA 95757
Phone: 916-686-9980

Emeryville # 072
5700 Christie Avenue
Emeryville, CA 94608
Phone: 510-658-8091

Encinitas # 025
115 N. El Camino Real,
Suite A
Encinitas, CA 92024
Phone: 760-634-2114

Encino # 056
17640 Burbank Blvd.
Encino, CA 91316
Phone: 818-990-7751

Escondido # 105
1885 So. Centre City
Pkwy., Unit "A"
Escondido, CA 92025
Phone: 760-233-4020

Fair Oaks # 071
5309 Sunrise Blvd.
Fair Oaks, CA 95628
Phone: 916-863-1744

Fairfield # 101
1350 Gateway Blvd.,
Suite A1-A7
Fairfield, CA 94533
Phone: 707-434-0144

Folsom # 172
850 East Bidwell
Folsom, CA 95630
Phone: 916-817-8820

Fremont # 077
39324 Argonaut Way
Fremont, CA 94538
Phone: 510-794-1386

Fresno # 008
5376 N. Blackstone
Fresno, CA 93710
Phone: 559-222-4348

Glendale # 053
130 N. Glendale Ave.
Glendale, CA 91206
Phone: 818-637-2990

Goleta # 110
5767 Calle Real
Goleta, CA 93117
Phone: 805-692-2234

Granada Hills # 044
11114 Balboa Blvd.
Granada Hills, CA 91344
Phone: 818-368-6461

Hollywood
1600 N. Vine Street
Los Angeles, CA 90028
Phone: 323-856-0689

Huntington Bch. # 047
18681-101 Main Street
Huntington Bch., CA 92648
Phone: 714-848-9640

Huntington Bch. # 241
21431 Brookhurst St.
Huntington Bch., CA 92646
Phone: 714-968-4070

Huntington Harbor # 244
Huntington Harbour Mall
16821 Algonquin St.
Huntington Bch., CA 92649
Phone: 714-846-7307

Irvine (Walnut Village Center) # 037
14443 Culver Drive
Irvine, CA 92604
Phone: 949-857-8108

Irvine (University Center) # 111
4225 Campus Dr.
Irvine, CA 92612
Phone: 949-509-6138

Irvine (Irvine & Sand Cyn) # 210
6222 Irvine Blvd.
Irvine, CA 92620
Phone: 949-551-6402

La Cañada # 042
475 Foothill Blvd.
La Canada, CA 91011
Phone: 818-790-6373

La Quinta # 189
46-400 Washington Street
La Quinta, CA 92253
Phone: 760-777-1553

Lafayette # 115
3649 Mt. Diablo Blvd.
Lafayette, CA 94549
Phone: 925-299-9344

Laguna Hills # 039
24321 Avenue De La Carlota
Laguna Hills, CA 92653
Phone: 949-586-8453

Laguna Niguel # 103
32351 Street of the Golden
Lantern
Laguna Niguel, CA 92677
Phone: 949-493-8599

La Jolla # 020
8657 Villa LaJolla
Drive #210
La Jolla, CA 92037
Phone: 858-546-8629

La Mesa # 024
5495 Grossmont Center Dr.
La Mesa, CA 91942
Phone: 619-466-0105

Larkspur # 235
2052 Redwood Hwy
Larkspur, CA 94921
Phone: 415-945-7955

Livermore # 208
1122-A East Stanley Blvd.
Livermore, CA 94550
Phone: 925-243-1947

Long Beach (PCH) # 043
6451 E. Pacific Coast Hwy.
Long Beach, CA 90803
Phone: 562-596-4388

Long Beach (Bellflower Blvd.) # 194
2222 Bellflower Blvd.
Long Beach, CA 90815
Phone: 562-596-2514

Los Altos # 127
2310 Homestead Rd.
Los Altos, CA 94024
Phone: 408-245-1917

Los Angeles (Silver Lake) # 017
2738 Hyperion Ave.
Los Angeles, CA 90027
Phone: 323-665-6774

Los Angeles # 031
263 S. La Brea
Los Angeles, CA 90036
Phone: 323-965-1989

Los Angeles (Sunset Strip) # 192
8000 Sunset Blvd.
Los Angeles, CA 90046
Phone: 323-822-7663

Los Gatos # 181
15466 Los Gatos Blvd.
Los Gatos, CA 95032
Phone 408-356-2324

Los Angeles (3rd & Fairfax)
W 3rd St. & S Fairfax Ave
Los Angeles, CA 90048
Phone: 323-931-4012

Manhattan Beach # 034
1821 Manhattan
Beach. Blvd.
Manhattan Bch., CA 90266
Phone: 310-372-1274

Manhattan Beach # 196
1800 Rosecrans Blvd.
Manhattan Beach,
CA 90266
Phone: 310-725-9800

Menlo Park # 069
720 Menlo Avenue
Menlo Park, CA 94025
Phone: 650-323-2134

Millbrae # 170
765 Broadway
Millbrae, CA 94030
Phone: 650-259-9142

Mission Viejo # 126
25410 Marguerite Parkway
Mission Viejo, CA 92692
Phone: 949-581-5638

Modesto # 009
3250 Dale Road
Modesto, CA 95356
Phone: 209-491-0445

Monrovia # 112
604 W. Huntington Dr.
Monrovia, CA 91016
Phone: 626-358-8884

Monterey # 204
570 Munras Ave., Ste. 20
Monterey, CA 93940
Phone: 831-372-2010

Montrose
2462 Honolulu Ave.
Montrose, CA 91020
Phone: 818-957-3613

Morgan Hill # 202
17035 Laurel Road
Morgan Hill, CA 95037
Phone: 408-778-6409

Mountain View # 081
590 Showers Dr.
Mountain View, CA 94040
Phone: 650-917-1013

Napa # 128
3654 Bel Aire Plaza
Napa, CA 94558
Phone: 707-256-0806

Newbury Park # 243
125 N. Reino Road
Newbury Park, CA
Phone: 805-375-1984

Newport Beach # 125
8086 East Coast Highway
Newport Beach, CA 92657
Phone: 949-494-7404

Novato # 198
7514 Redwood Blvd.
Novato, CA 94945
Phone: 415-898-9359

**Oakland
(Lakeshore) # 203**
3250 Lakeshore Ave.
Oakland, CA 94610
Phone: 510-238-9076

Oakland (Rockridge) # 231
5727 College Ave.
Oakland, CA 94618
Phone: 510-923-9428

Oceanside # 22
2570 Vista Way
Oceanside, CA 92054
Phone: 760-433-9994

Orange # 046
2114 N. Tustin St.
Orange, CA 92865
Phone: 714-283-5697

Pacific Grove # 008
1170 Forest Avenue
Pacific Grove, CA 93950
Phone: 831-656-0180

Palm Desert # 003
44-250 Town Center Way,
Suite C6
Palm Desert, CA 92260
Phone: 760-340-2291

Palmdale # 185
39507 10th Street West
Palmdale, CA 93551
Phone: 661-947-2890

Palo Alto # 207
855 El Camino Real
Palo Alto, CA 94301
Phone: 650-327-7018

**Pasadena
(S. Lake Ave.) # 179**
345 South Lake Ave.
Pasadena, CA 91101
Phone: 626-395-9553

**Pasadena
(S. Arroyo Pkwy.) # 051**
610 S. Arroyo Parkway
Pasadena, CA 91105
Phone: 626-568-9254

**Pasadena
(Hastings Ranch) # 171**
467 Rosemead Blvd.
Pasadena, CA 91107
Phone: 626-351-3399

Petaluma # 107
169 North McDowell Blvd.
Petaluma, CA 94954
Phone: 707-769-2782

Pinole # 230
2742 Pinole Valley Rd.
Pinole, CA 94564
Phone: 510-222-3501

Pleasanton # 066
4040 Pimlico #150
Pleasanton, CA 94588
Phone: 925-225-3600

Rancho Cucamonga # 217
6401 Haven Ave.
Rancho Cucamonga,
CA 91737
Phone: 909-476-1410

Rancho Palos Verdes # 057
28901 S. Western Ave. #243
Rancho Palos Verdes,
CA 90275
Phone: 310-832-1241

Rancho Palos Verdes # 233
31176 Hawthorne Blvd.
Rancho Palos Verdes, CA
90275
Phone: 310-544-1727

**Rancho Santa
Margarita # 027**
30652 Santa Margarita Pkwy.
Suite F102
Rancho Santa Margarita,
CA 92688
Phone: 949-888-3640

Redding # 219
845 Browning St.
Redding, CA 96003
Phone: 530-223-4875

Redlands # 099
552 Orange Street Plaza
Redlands, CA 92374
Phone: 909-798-3888

Redondo Beach # 038
1761 S. Elena Avenue
Redondo Bch., CA 90277
Phone: 310-316-1745

Riverside # 15
6225 Riverside Plaza
Riverside, CA 92506
Phone: 951-682-4684

Roseville # 80
1117 Roseville Square
Roseville, CA 95678
Phone: 916-784-9084

**Sacramento
(Folsom Blvd.) # 175**
5000 Folsom Blvd.
Sacramento, CA 95819
Phone: 916-456-1853

**Sacramento
(Fulton & Marconi) # 070**
2625 Marconi Avenue
Sacramento, CA 95821
Phone: 916-481-8797

San Carlos # 174
1482 El Camino Real
San Carlos, CA 94070
Phone: 650-594-2138

San Clemente # 016
638 Camino DeLosMares,
Sp.#115-G
San Clemente, CA 92673
Phone: 949-240-9996

**San Diego
(Hillcrest) # 026**
1090 University Ste.
G100-107
San Diego, CA 92103
Phone: 619-296-3122

**San Diego
(Point Loma) # 188**
2401 Truxtun Rd., Ste. 300
San Diego, CA 92106
Phone: 619-758-9272

**San Diego
(Pacific Beach) # 021**
1211 Garnet Avenue
San Diego, CA 92109
Phone: 858-272-7235

**San Diego (Carmel
Mtn. Ranch) # 023**
11955 Carmel Mtn. Rd. #702
San Diego, CA 92128
Phone: 858-673-0526

**San Diego
(Scripps Ranch) # 221**
9850 Hibert Street
San Diego, CA 92131
Phone: 858-549-9185

San Dimas # 028
856 Arrow Hwy. "C"
Target Center
San Dimas, CA 91773
Phone: 909-305-4757

**San Francisco
(9th Street) # 078**
555 9th Street
San Francisco, CA 94103
Phone: 415-863-1292

**San Francisco
(Masonic Ave.) # 100**
3 Masonic Avenue
San Francisco, CA 94118
Phone: 415-346-9964

San Francisco (Nob Hill)
1095 Hyde St.
San Francisco, CA 94109
Phone: 415-292-7665

**San Francisco
(North Beach) #019**
410 Bay Street
San Francisco, CA 94133
Phone: 415-351-1013

**San Francisco
(Stonestown) # 236**
265 Winston Dr.
San Francisco, CA 94132
Phone: 415-665-1835

San Gabriel # 032
7260 N. Rosemead Blvd.
San Gabriel, CA 91775
Phone: 626-285-5862

San Jose (Bollinger) # 232
7250 Bollinger Rd.
San Jose, CA 95129
Phone: 408-873-7384

**San Jose
(Coleman Ave) # 212**
635 Coleman Ave.
San Jose, CA 95110
Phone: 408-298-9731

**San Jose
(Old Almaden) # 063**
5353 Almaden Expressway
#J-38
San Jose, CA 95118
Phone: 408-927-9091

**San Jose
(Westgate West) # 062**
5269 Prospect
San Jose, CA 95129
Phone: 408-446-5055

San Luis Obispo # 041
3977 Higuera Street
San Luis Obispo, CA 93401
Phone: 805-783-2780

**San Mateo
(Grant Street) # 067**
1820-22 S. Grant Street
San Mateo, CA 94402
Phone: 650-570-6140

**San Mateo
(Hillsdale) # 245**
45 W Hillsdale Blvd
San Mateo, CA 94403
Phone: 650-286-1509

San Rafael # 061
337 Third Street
San Rafael, CA 94901
Phone: 415-454-9530

Santa Ana # 113
3329 South Bristol Street
Santa Ana, CA 92704
Phone: 714-424-9304

**Santa Barbara
(S. Milpas St.) # 059**
29 S. Milpas Street
Santa Barbara, CA 93103
Phone: 805-564-7878

**Santa Barbara
(De La Vina) # 183**
3025 De La Vina
Santa Barbara, CA 93105
Phone: 805-563-7383

Santa Cruz # 193
700 Front Street
Santa Cruz, CA 95060
Phone: 831-425-0140

Santa Maria # 239
1303 S. Bradley Road
Santa Maria, CA 93454
Phone: 805-925-1657

Santa Monica # 006
3212 Pico Blvd.
Santa Monica, CA 90405
Phone: 310-581-0253

**Santa Rosa
(Cleveland Ave.) # 075**
3225 Cleveland Avenue
Santa Rosa, CA 95403
Phone: 707-525-1406

**Santa Rosa
(Santa Rosa Ave.) # 178**
2100 Santa Rosa Ave.
Santa Rosa, CA 95407
Phone: 707-535-0788

Sherman Oaks # 049
14119 Riverside Drive
Sherman Oaks, CA 91423
Phone: 818-789-2771

Simi Valley # 030
2975-A Cochran St.
Simi Valley, CA 93065
Phone: 805-520-3135

South Pasadena # 018
613 Mission Street
South Pasadena, CA 91030
Phone: 626-441-6263

South San Francisco # 187
301 McLellan Dr.
So. San Francisco,
CA 94080
Phone: 650-583-6401

Stockton # 076
6535 Pacific Avenue
Stockton, CA 95207
Phone: 209-951-7597

Studio City # 122
11976 Ventura Blvd.
Studio City, CA 91604
Phone: 818-509-0168

Sunnyvale # 068
727 Sunnyvale/
Saratoga Rd.
Sunnyvale, CA 94087
Phone: 408-481-9082

Temecula # 102
40665 Winchester Rd.,
Bldg. B, Ste. 4-6
Temecula, CA 92591
Phone: 951-296-9964

Templeton # 211
1111 Rossi Road
Templeton, CA 93465
Phone: 805-434-9562

Thousand Oaks # 196
451 Avenida
De Los Arboles
Thousand Oaks, CA 91360
Phone: 805-492-7107

Toluca Lake # 054
10130 Riverside Drive
Toluca Lake, CA 91602
Phone: 818-762-2787

**Torrance
(Hawthorne Blvd.) # 121**
19720 Hawthorne Blvd.
Torrance, CA 90503
Phone: 310-793-8585

**Torrance (Rolling
Hills Plaza) # 029**
2545 Pacific Coast Highway
Torrance, CA 90505
Phone: 310-326-9520

Tustin # 197
12932 Newport Avenue
Tustin, CA 92780
Phone: 714-669-3752

Upland # 010
333 So. Mountain Avenue
Upland, CA 91786
Phone: 909-946-4799

Valencia # 013
26517 Bouquet Canyon Rd
Santa Clarita, CA 91350
Phone: 661-263-3796

Ventura # 045
1795 S. Victoria Avenue
Ventura, CA 93003
Phone: 805-650-9977

Ventura – Midtown
103 S. Mills Road Suite 104
Ventura, CA 93003
Phone: 805-658-2664

Walnut Creek # 123
1372 So. California Blvd.
Walnut Creek, CA 94596
Phone: 925-945-1674

West Hills # 050
6751 Fallbrook Ave.
West Hills, CA 91307
Phone: 818-347-2591

West Hollywood # 040
7304 Santa Monica Blvd.
West Hollywood, CA 90046
Phone: 323-851-9772

West Hollywood # 173
8611 Santa Monica Blvd.
West Hollywood, CA 90069
Phone: 310-657-0152

**West Los Angeles
(National Blvd.) # 007**
10850 National Blvd.
West Los Angeles, CA 90064
Phone: 310-470-1917

**West Los Angeles
S. Sepulveda Blvd.) # 119**
3456 S. Sepulveda Blvd.
West Los Angeles, CA 90034
Phone: 310-836-2458

**West Los Angeles
(Olympic) # 215**
11755 W. Olympic Blvd.
West Los Angeles,
CA 90064
Phone: 310-477-5949

Westchester # 033
8645 S. Sepulveda
Westchester, CA 90045
Phone: 310-338-9238

Westlake Village # 058
3835 E. Thousand
Oaks Blvd.
Westlake Village, CA 91362
Phone: 805-494-5040

Westwood # 234
1000 Glendon Avenue
Los Angeles, CA 90024
Phone: 310-824-1495

Whittier # 048
15025 E. Whittier Blvd.
Whittier, CA 90603
Phone: 562-698-1642

Woodland Hills # 209
21054 Clarendon St.
Woodland Hills, CA 91364
Phone: 818-712-9475

Yorba Linda # 176
19655 Yorba Linda Blvd.
Yorba Linda, CA 92886
Phone: 714-970-0116

Connecticut

Danbury # 525
113 Mill Plain Rd.
Danbury, CT 06811
Phone: 203-739-0098
Alcohol: Beer Only

Darien # 522
436 Boston Post Rd.
Darien, CT 06820
Phone: 203-656-1414
Alcohol: Beer Only

Fairfield # 523
2258 Black Rock Turnpike
Fairfield, CT 06825
Phone: 203-330-8301
Alcohol: Beer Only

Orange # 524
560 Boston Post Road
Orange, CT 06477
Phone: 203-795-5505
Alcohol: Beer Only

West Hartford # 526
1489 New Britain Ave.
West Hartford, CT 06110
Phone: 860-561-4771
Alcohol: Beer Only

Westport # 521
400 Post Road East
Westport, CT 06880
Phone: 203-226-8966
Alcohol: Beer Only

Delaware

Wilmington* # 536
5605 Concord Pike
Wilmington, DE 19803
Phone: 302-478-8494

District of Columbia

Washington # 653
1101 25th Street NW
Washington, DC 20037
Phone: 202-296-1921

Florida

Gainesville – Coming Soon!
3724 SW Archer Rd.
Gainesville, GL 32608
Phone: TBD

Naples
10600 Tamiami Trail North
Naples, FL 34108
Phone: 239-596-5631

Sarasota
4101 S. Tamiami Trail
Sarasota, FL 34231
Phone: 941-922-5727

Georgia

Athens
1850 Epps Bridge Parkway
Athens, GA 30606
Phone: 706-583-8934

**Atlanta
(Buckhead) # 735**
3183 Peachtree Rd NE
Atlanta, GA 30305
Phone: 404-842-0907

Atlanta (Midtown) # 730
931 Monroe Dr., NE
Atlanta, GA 30308
Phone: 404-815-9210

Marietta # 732
4250 Roswell Road
Marietta, GA 30062
Phone: 678-560-3585

Norcross # 734
5185 Peachtree Parkway,
Bld. 1200
Norcross, GA 30092
Phone: 678-966-9236

Roswell # 733
635 W. Crossville Road
Roswell, GA 30075
Phone: 770-645-8505

Sandy Springs # 731
6277 Roswell Road NE
Sandy Springs, GA 30328
Phone: 404-236-2414

Illinois

Algonquin # 699
1800 South Randall Road
Algonquin, IL 60102
Phone: 847-854-4886

Arlington Heights # 687
17 W. Rand Road
Arlington Heights, IL 60004
Phone: 847-506-0752

Batavia # 689
1942 West Fabyan
Parkway #222
Batavia, IL 60510
Phone: 630-879-3234

Chicago (Diversey Pkwy)
667 W. Diversey Pkwy
Chicago, IL 60614
Phone: 773-935-7255

**Chicago
(Lincoln & Grace) # 688**
3745 North Lincoln Avenue
Chicago, IL 60613
Phone: 773-248-4920

**Chicago
(Lincoln Park) # 691**
1840 North Clybourn
Avenue #200
Chicago, IL 60614
Phone: 312-274-9733

**Chicago
(River North) # 696**
44 E. Ontario St.
Chicago, IL 60611
Phone: 312-951-6369

Chicago (South Loop)
1147 S. Wabash Ave.
Chicago, IL 60605
Phone: 312-588-0489

Downers Grove # 683
122 Ogden Ave.
Downers Grove, IL 60515
Phone: 630-241-1662

Glen Ellyn # 680
680 Roosevelt Rd.
Glen Ellyn, IL 60137
Phone: 630-858-5077

Glenview # 681
1407 Waukegan Road
Glenview, IL 60025
Phone: 847-657-7821

La Grange # 685
25 North La Grange Road
La Grange, IL 60525
Phone: 708-579-0838

Lake Zurich # 684
735 W. Route 22**
Lake Zurich, IL 60047
Phone: 847-550-7827
[**For accurate driving
directions using
GPS, please use
735 W Main Street]

Naperville # 690
44 West Gartner Road
Naperville, IL 60540
Phone: 630-355-4389

Northbrook # 682
127 Skokie Blvd.
Northbrook, IL 60062
Phone: 847-498-9076

Oak Park # 697
483 N. Harlem Ave.
Oak Park, IL 60301
Phone: 708-386-1169

Orland Park # 686
14924 S. La Grange Road
Orland Park, IL 60462
Phone: 708-349-9021

Park Ridge # 698
190 North Northwest Hwy
Park Ridge, IL 60068
Phone: 847-292-1108

Indiana

**Indianapolis
(Castleton) # 671**
5473 East 82nd Street
Indianapolis, IN 46250
Phone: 317-595-8950

**Indianapolis
(West 86th) # 670**
2902 West 86th Street
Indianapolis, IN 46268
Phone: 317-337-1880

Iowa

West Des Moines
6305 Mills Civic Parkway
West Des Moines, IA 50266
Phone: 515-225-3820

Kansas

Leawood* #723
4201 W 119th Street
Leawood, KS 66209
Phone: 913-327-7209

Kentucky

Louisville
4600 Shelbyville Road
Louisville, KY 40207
Phone: 502-895-1361

Lexington Grocery
2326 Nicholasville Rd
Lexington, KY 40503
Phone: 859-313-5030

Lexington Wine
2320 Nicholasville Rd
Lexington, KY 40503
Phone: 859-277-0144

Maine

Portland # 519
87 Marginal Way
Portland, ME 04101
Phone: 207-699-3799

Maryland

Annapolis* # 650
160 F Jennifer Road
Annapolis, MD 21401
Phone: 410-573-0505

Bethesda* # 645
6831 Wisconsin Avenue
Bethesda, MD 20815
Phone: 301-907-0982

Columbia* # 658
6610 Marie Curie Dr.
(Int. of 175 & 108)
Elkridge, MD 21075
Phone: 410-953-8139

Gaithersburg* # 648
18270 Contour Rd.
Gaithersburg, MD 20877
Phone: 301-947-5953

Pikesville* # 655
1809 Reisterstown Road,
Suite #121
Pikesville, MD 21208
Phone: 410-484-8373

Rockville* # 642
12268-H Rockville Pike
Rockville, MD 20852
Phone: 301-468-6656

Silver Spring* # 652
10741 Columbia Pike
Silver Spring, MD 20901
Phone: 301-681-1675

Towson* # 649
1 E. Joppa Rd.
Towson, MD 21286
Phone: 410-296-9851

Massachusetts

Acton* # 511
145 Great Road
Acton, MA 01720
Phone: 978-266-8908

Arlington* # 505
1427 Massachusetts Ave.
Arlington, MA 02476
Phone: 781-646-9138

Boston #510
899 Boylston Street
Boston, MA 02115
Phone: 617-262-6505

Brookline # 501
1317 Beacon Street
Brookline, MA 02446
Phone: 617-278-9997

Burlington* # 515
51 Middlesex Turnpike
Burlington, MA 01803
Phone: 781-273-2310

Cambridge
748 Memorial Drive
Cambridge, MA 02139
Phone: 617-491-8582

**Cambridge
(Fresh Pond)* # 517**
211 Alewife Brook Pkwy
Cambridge, MA 02138
Phone: 617-498-3201

Framingham # 503
659 Worcester Road
Framingham, MA 01701
Phone: 508-935-2931

Hadley* # 512
375 Russell Street
Hadley, MA 01035
Phone: 413-587-3260

Hanover* # 513
1775 Washington Street
Hanover, MA 02339
Phone: 781-826-5389

Hyannis* # 514
Christmas Tree Promenade
655 Route 132, Unit 4-A
Hyannis, MA 02601
Phone: 508-790-3008

Needham Hts* 504
958 Highland Avenue
Needham Hts, MA 02494
Phone: 781-449-6993

Peabody* # 516
300 Andover Street,
Suite 15
Peabody, MA 01960
Phone: 978-977-5316

Saugus* # 506
358 Broadway, Unit B
(Shops @ Saugus, Rte. 1)
Saugus, MA 01906
Phone: 781-231-0369

Shrewsbury* # 508
77 Boston Turnpike
Shrewsbury, MA 01545
Phone: 508-755-9560

West Newton* # 509
1121 Washington St.
West Newton, MA 02465
Phone: 617-244-1620

Michigan

Ann Arbor # 678
2398 East Stadium Blvd.
Ann Arbor, MI 48104
Phone: 734-975-2455

Farmington Hills # 675
31221 West 14 Mile Road
Farmington Hills, MI 48334
Phone: 248-737-4609

Grosse Pointe # 665
17028 Kercheval Ave.
Grosse Pointe, MI 48230
Phone: 313-640-7794

Northville # 667
20490 Haggerty Road
Northville, MI 48167
Phone: 734-464-3675

Rochester Hills # 668
3044 Walton Blvd.
Rochester Hills, MI 48309
Phone: 248-375-2190

Royal Oak # 674
27880 Woodward Ave.
Royal Oak, MI 48067
Phone: 248-582-9002

Minnesota

Bloomington
4270 W. 78th St.
Bloomington, MN 55435
Phone: 952-835-8640

Maple Grove # 713
12105 Elm Creek Blvd. N.
Maple Grove, MN 55369
Phone: 763-315-1739

Minnetonka # 714
11220 Wayzata Blvd
Minnetonka, MN 55305
Phone: 952-417-9080

Rochester
1200 16th St. SW
Rochester, NY 55902
Phone: 952-417-9080

St. Louis Park # 710
4500 Excelsior Blvd.
St. Louis Park, MN 55416
Phone: 952-285-1053

St. Paul # 716
484 Lexington Parkway S.
St. Paul, MN 55116
Phone: 651-698-3119

Woodbury # 715
8960 Hudson Road
Woodbury, MN 55125
Phone: 651-735-0269

Missouri

Brentwood # 792
48 Brentwood
Promenade Court
Brentwood, MO 63144
Phone: 314-963-0253

Chesterfield # 693
1679 Clarkson Road
Chesterfield, MO 63017
Phone: 636-536-7846

Creve Coeur # 694
11505 Olive Blvd.
Creve Coeur, MO 63141
Phone: 314-569-0427

Des Peres # 695
13343 Manchester Rd.
Des Peres, MO 63131
Phone: 314-984-5051

Kansas City
8600 Ward Parkway
Kansas City, MO 64114
Phone: 816-333-5322

Nebraska

Lincoln
3120 Pine Lake Road, Suite R
Lincoln, NE 68516
Phone: 402-328-0120

Omaha # 714
10305 Pacific St.
Omaha, NE 68114
Phone: 402-391-3698

Nevada

Anthem # 280
10345 South Eastern Ave.
Henderson, NV 89052
Phone: 702-407-8673

Carson City # 281
3790 US Highway 395 S,
Suite 401
Carson City, NV 89705
Phone: 775-267-2486

Henderson # 097
2716 North Green Valley
Parkway
Henderson, NV 89014
Phone: 702-433-6773

**Las Vegas
(Decatur Blvd.) # 098**
2101 S. Decatur Blvd., Suite 25
Las Vegas, NV 89102
Phone: 702-367-0227

Las Vegas (Summerlin) # 086
7575 West Washington,
Suite 117
Las Vegas, NV 89128
Phone: 702-242-8240

Reno # 082
5035 S. McCarran Blvd.
Reno, NV 89502
Phone: 775-826-1621

New Hampshire

Nashua – Coming Soon!
262 Daniel Webster Hwy
Nashua, NH 03060
Phone: TBD

*Newington (Portsmouth) –
Coming Soon!*
45 Gosling Rd
Newington, NH 03801
Phone: TBD

New Jersey

Edgewater* # 606
715 River Road
Edgewater, NJ 07020
Phone: 201-945-5932

Florham Park* # 604
186 Columbia Turnpike
Florham Park, NJ 07932
Phone: 973-514-1511

Marlton* # 631
300 P Route 73 South
Marlton, NJ 08053
Phone: 856-988-3323

Millburn* # 609
187 Millburn Ave.
Millburn, NJ 07041
Phone: 973-218-0912

Paramus* # 605
404 Rt. 17 North
Paramus, NJ 07652
Phone: 201-265-9624

Princeton # 607
3528 US 1
(Brunswick Pike)
Princeton, NJ 08540
Phone: 609-897-0581

Shrewsbury*
1031 Broad St.
Shrewsbury, NJ 07702
Phone: 732-389-2535

Wayne* # 632
1172 Hamburg Turnpike
Wayne, NJ 07470
Phone: 973-692-0050

Westfield # 601
155 Elm St.
Westfield, NJ 07090
Phone: 908-301-0910

Westwood* # 602
20 Irvington Street
Westwood, NJ 07675
Phone: 201-263-0134

New Mexico

Albuquerque # 166
8928 Holly Ave. NE
Albuquerque, NM 87122
Phone: 505-796-0311

**Albuquerque
(Uptown) # 167**
2200 Uptown Loop NE
Albuquerque, NM 87110
Phone: 505-883-3662

Santa Fe # 165
530 W. Cordova Road
Santa Fe, NM 87505
Phone: 505-995-8145

New York

NY stores sell beer only

Brooklyn # 558
130 Court St
Brooklyn, NY 11201
Phone: 718-246-8460

Colonie (Albany)
79 Wolf Road
Colonie, NY 12205
Phone: 51-482-4538

Commack # 551
5010 Jericho Turnpike
Commack, NY 11725
Phone: 631-493-9210

Store does not carry alcohol

Hartsdale # 533
215 North Central Avenue
Hartsdale, NY 10530
Phone: 914-997-1960

Hewlett # 554
1280 West Broadway
Hewlett, NY 11557
Phone: 516-569-7191

Lake Grove # 556
137 Alexander Ave.
Lake Grove, NY 11755
Phone: 631-863-2477

Larchmont # 532
1260 Boston Post Road
Larchmont, NY 10538
Phone: 914-833-9110

Merrick # 553
1714 Merrick Road
Merrick, NY 11566
Phone: 516-771-1012

**New York
(72nd & Broadway) # 542**
2075 Broadway
New York, NY 10023
Phone: 212-799-0028

**New York
(Chelsea) # 543**
675 6th Ave
New York, NY 10010
Phone: 212-255-2106

**New York (Union Square
Grocery) # 540**
142 E. 14th St.
New York, NY 10003
Phone: 212-529-4612

**New York (Union Square
Wine) # 541**
138 E. 14th St.
New York, NY 10003
Phone: 212-529-6326
Alcohol: Wine Only

Oceanside # 552
3418 Long Beach Rd.
Oceanside, NY 11572
Phone: 516-536-9163

Plainview # 555
425 S. Oyster Bay Rd.
Plainview, NY 11803
Phone: 516-933-6900

Queens # 557
90-30 Metropolitan Ave.
Queens, NY 11374
Phone: 718-275-1791

Rochester
3349 Monroe Ave
Rochester, NY 14618
Phone: 585-248-5011

Scarsdale # 531
727 White Plains Rd.
Scarsdale, NY 10583
Phone: 914-472-2988

Staten Island
2385 Richmond Ave
Staten Island, NY 10314
Phone: 718-370-1085

Westbury
900 Old Country Road
Garden City, NY 11530
Phone: Phone# 516-794-0174

North Carolina

Cary # 741
1393 Kildaire Farms Rd.
Cary, NC 27511
Phone: 919-465-5984

Chapel Hill # 745
1800 E. Franklin St.
Chapel Hill, NC 27514
Phone: 919-918-7871

**Charlotte
(Midtown) # 744**
1133 Metropolitan Ave.,
Ste. 100
Charlotte, NC 28204
Phone: 704-334-0737

Charlotte (North) # 743
1820 East Arbors Dr.**
(corner of W. Mallard Creek
Church Rd. & Senator
Royall Dr.)
Charlotte, NC 28262
Phone: 704-688-9578
[**For accurate driving
directions on the web, please
use 1820 W. Mallard Creek
Church Rd.]

Charlotte (South) # 742
6418 Rea Rd.
Charlotte, NC 28277
Phone: 704-543-5249

Raleigh # 746
3000 Wake Forest Rd.
Raleigh, NC 27609
Phone: 919-981-7422

Wilmington
1437 S. College Road
Wilmington, NC 28403
Phone: 919-981-7422

Winston-Salem
252 S. Stratford Road
Winston Salem, NC 27103
Phone: 336-721-1744

Ohio

Cincinnati # 669
7788 Montgomery Road
Cincinnati, OH 45236
Phone: 513-984-3452

Columbus # 679
3888 Townsfair Way
Columbus, OH 43219
Phone: 614-473-0794

Dublin # 672
6355 Sawmill Road
Dublin, OH 43017
Phone: 614-793-8505

Kettering # 673
328 East Stroop Road
Kettering, OH 45429
Phone: 937-294-5411

Westlake # 677
175 Market Street
Westlake, OH 44145
Phone: 440-250-1592

Woodmere # 676
28809 Chagrin Blvd.
Woodmere, OH 44122
Phone: 216-360-9320

Oregon

Beaverton # 141
11753 S. W. Beaverton
Hillsdale Hwy.
Beaverton, OR 97005
Phone: 503-626-3794

Bend # 150
63455 North
Highway 97, Ste. 4
Bend, OR 97701
Phone: 541-312-4198

Clackamas # 152
9345 SE 82nd Ave (across
from Home Depot)
Happy Valley, OR 97086
Phone: 503-771-6300

Corvallis # 154
1550 NW 9th Street
Corvallis, OR 97330
Phone: 541-753-0048

Eugene # 145
85 Oakway Center
Eugene, OR 97401
Phone: 541-485-1744

Hillsboro # 149
2285 NW 185th Ave.
Hillsboro, OR 97124
Phone: 503-645-8321

Lake Oswego # 142
15391 S. W. Bangy Rd.
Lake Oswego, OR 97035
Phone: 503-639-3238

Medford
Northgate Marketplace
1500 Court St.
Medford, OR 97501
Phone: 541-608-4993

Portland (SE) # 143
4715 S. E. 39th Avenue
Portland, OR 97202
Phone: 503-777-1601

Portland (NW) # 146
2122 N.W. Glisan
Portland, OR 97210
Phone: 971-544-0788

**Portland
(Hollywood) # 144**
4121 N.E. Halsey St.
Portland, OR 97213
Phone: 503-284-1694

Salem #153
4450 Commercial St.,
Suite 100
Salem, OR 97302
Phone: 503-378-9042

Pennsylvania

Ardmore* # 635
112 Coulter Avenue
Ardmore, PA 19003
Phone: 610-658-0645

Jenkintown* # 633
933 Old York Road
Jenkintown, PA 19046
Phone: 215-885-524

Media* # 637
12 East State Street
Media, PA 19063
Phone: 610-891-2752

North Wales* # 639
1430 Bethlehem Pike
(corner SR 309 & SR 63)
North Wales, PA 19454
Phone: 215-646-5870

Philadelphia* # 634
2121 Market Street
Philadelphia, PA 19103
Phone: 215-569-9282

Pittsburgh* # 638
6343 Penn Ave.
Pittsburgh, PA 15206
Phone: 412-363-5748

Pittsburgh*
1630 Washington Road
Pittsburgh, PA 15228
Phone: 412-835-2212

State College*
1855 North Atherton St.
State College, PA 16803
Phone: 814-234-2224

Store does not carry alcohol   269

Wayne* # 632
171 East Swedesford Rd.
Wayne, PA 19087
Phone: 610-225-0925

Rhode Island

Warwick* # 518
1000 Bald Hill Rd
Warwick, RI 02886
Phone: 401-821-5368

South Carolina

Columbia – Coming Soon!
4502 Forest Drive
Columbia, SC 29206
Phone: TBD

Greenville
59 Woodruff
Industrial Lane
Greenville, SC 29607
Phone: 864-286-0231

Mt. Pleasant – #752
401 Johnnie Dodds Blvd.
Mt. Pleasant, SC 29464
Phone: 843-884-4037

Tennessee

Knoxville
8025 Kingston Pike
Knoxville, TN 37919
Phone: 865-670-4088
Alcohol: Beer Only

Nashville # 664
3909 Hillsboro Pike
Nashville, TN 37215
Phone: 615-297-6560
Alcohol: Beer Only

Texas

Austin – Coming Soon!
211 Seaholm Dr, Ste 100
Austin, TX 78703

*Dallas (Lower Greenville) –
Coming Soon!*
2001 Greenville Ave
Dallas, TX 75206

*Dallas (Preston Hallow
Village) – Coming Soon!*
Central Expy & Walnut
Hill Ln

Fort Worth
2701 S. Hulen St
For Worth, TX 76107
Phone: 817-922-9107

Houston (Alabama Theater)
2922 S Shepherd Dr
Houston, TX 77098
Phone: 713-526-4034

*Houston (Memorial Area) –
Coming Soon!*
1440 S Voss Road
Houston, TX 77057

Plano
2400 Preston Rd Ste 200
Plano, TX 75093
Phone: 972-312-9538

San Antonio – Coming Soon!
350 East Basse Rd
San Antonio, TX 78209

The Woodlands
10868 Kuykendahl Road
The Woodlands, TX 77381
Phone: 281-465-0254

Utah

*Salt Lake City –
Coming Soon!*
634 East 400 South
Salt Lake City, UT 84102
Phone: TBD

Virginia

Alexandria # 647
612 N. Saint Asaph Street
Alexandria, VA 22314
Phone: 703-548-0611

Bailey's Crossroads # 644
5847 Leesburg Pike
Bailey's Crossroads,
VA 22041
Phone: 703-379-5883

Centreville # 654
14100 Lee Highway
Centreville, VA 20120
Phone: 703-815-0697

Charlottesville
2025 Bond St.
Charlottesville, VA 22901
Phone: 434-974-1466

Clarendon
1109 N. Highland St.
Arlington, VA 22201
Phone: 703-351-8015

Fairfax # 643
9464 Main Street
Fairfax, VA 22031
Phone: 703-764-8550

Falls Church # 641
7514 Leesburg Turnpike
Falls Church, VA 22043
Phone: 703-288-0566

Newport News # 656
12551 Jefferson Ave.,
Suite #179
Newport News, VA 23602
Phone: 757-890-0235

Reston # 646
11958 Killingsworth Ave.
Reston, VA 20194
Phone: 703-689-0865

**Richmond
(Short Pump) # 659**
11331 W Broad St, Ste 161
Glen Allen, VA 23060
Phone: 804-360-4098

Springfield # 651
6394 Springfield Plaza
Springfield, VA 22150
Phone: 703-569-9301

Virginia Beach # 660
503 Hilltop Plaza
Virginia Beach, VA 23454
Phone: 757-422-4840

Williamsburg # 657
5000 Settlers Market Blvd
(corner of Monticello and
Settlers Market)**
Williamsburg, VA 23188
Phone: 757-259-2135
[**For accurate driving
directions on the web, please
use 5224 Monticello Ave.]

Washington

Ballard # 147
4609 14th Avenue NW
Seattle, WA 98107
Phone: 206-783-0498

Bellevue # 131
15400 N. E. 20th Street
Bellevue, WA 98007
Phone: 425-643-6885

Bellingham # 151
2410 James Street
Bellingham, WA 98225
Phone: 360-734-5166

Burien # 133
15868 1st. Avenue South
Burien, WA 98148
Phone: 206-901-9339

Everett # 139
811 S.E. Everett Mall Way
Everett, WA 98208
Phone: 425-513-2210

Federal Way # 134
1758 S. 320th Street
Federal Way, WA 98003
Phone: 253-529-9242

Issaquah # 138
1495 11th Ave. N.W.
Issaquah, WA 98027
Phone: 425-837-8088

Kirkland # 132
12632 120th Avenue N. E.
Kirkland, WA 98034
Phone: 425-823-1685

Lynnwood # 129
19500 Highway 99,
Suite 100
Lynnwood, WA 98036
Phone: 425-744-1346

Olympia # 156
Olympia West Center
1530 Black Lake Blvd.
Olympia, WA 98502
Phone: 360-352-744

Redmond # 140
15932 Redmond Way
Redmond, WA 98052
Phone: 425-883-1624

Seattle (U. District) # 137
4555 Roosevelt Way NE
Seattle, WA 98105
Phone: 206-547-6299

**Seattle
(Queen Anne Hill) # 135**
112 West Galer St.
Seattle, WA 98119
Phone: 206-378-5536

Seattle (Capitol Hill) # 130
1700 Madison St.
Seattle, WA 98122
Phone: 206-322-7268

Seattle (West)
4545 Fauntleroy Way SW
Seattle, WA 98116
Phone: 206-913-0013

Silverdale
9991 Mickelberry Rd.
Silverdale, WA 98383
Phone: 360-307-7224

Spokane
2975 East 29th Avenue
Spokane, WA 99223
Phone: 509-534-1077

University Place # 148
3800 Bridgeport Way West
University Place, WA 98466
Phone: 253-460-2672

Vancouver # 136
305 SE Chkalov Drive #B1
Vancouver, WA 98683
Phone: 360-883-9000

Wisconsin

Brookfield
12665 W. Bluemound Rd
Brookfield, WI 53005
Phone: 262-784-4806

Glendale # 711
5600 North Port
Washington Road
Glendale, WI 53217
Phone: 414-962-3382

Madison # 712
1810 Monroe Street
Madison, WI 53711
Phone: 608-257-1916

Although we aim to ensure that the store location information contained here is correct, we will not be responsible for any errors or omissions.

Photo / Image Credits

Photography of recipes © Deana Gunn and Wona Miniati

Other titles in this cookbook series:

Cooking with All Things Trader Joe's
by Deana Gunn & Wona Miniati
ISBN 978-0-9799384-8-1

Cooking with Trader Joe's: Companion
by Deana Gunn & Wona Miniati
ISBN 978-0-9799384-9-8

Cooking with Trader Joe's: Dinner's Done!
by Deana Gunn & Wona Miniati
ISBN 978-0-9799384-3-6

Cooking with Trader Joe's: Pack A Lunch!
by Céline Cossou-Bordes
ISBN 978-0-9799384-5-0

Cooking with Trader Joe's: Skinny Dish! (Vegan)
by Jennifer K. Reilly, RD
ISBN 978-0-9799384-7-4

Cooking with Trader Joe's: Lighten Up!
by Susan Greeley, MS, RD
ISBN 978-0-9799384-6-7

Cooking with Trader Joe's: Easy Lunch Boxes
by Kelly Lester
ISBN 978-1-938706-00-4

Cooking with Trader Joe's: Gluten-Free
by Deana Gunn & Wona Miniati
ISBN 978-1-938706-02-8

Available everywhere books are sold.
Please visit us at

CookTJ.com